# The Basic Book of

# Graphic Arts

Robert M. Swerdlow

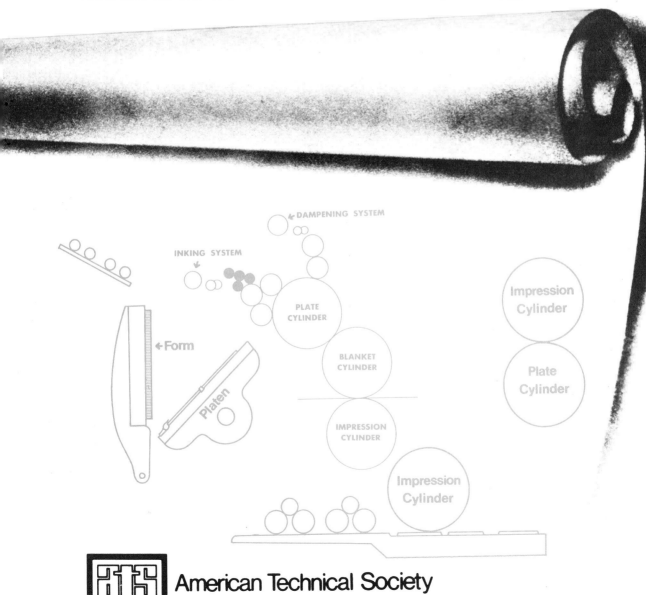

American Technical Society
CHICAGO, ILL. 60637

# CONTENTS

# PREFACE

THE BASIC BOOK OF GRAPHIC ARTS is part of an integrated series of Industrial Arts textbooks designed to teach basic skills to beginning students. Its major objectives are: career exploration, and development of consumer awareness, manipulative skills, and craftsmanship. The philosophy of THE BASIC BOOK OF GRAPHIC ARTS is based on a recent, nationwide survey in which graphic arts teachers at all levels were asked to outline the courses they taught and let us know what types of instructional materials they actually needed. The result is a highly-visual text with a controlled reading level that will help insure student success.

The author and the publisher wish to acknowledge and thank the following corporations for their assistance and cooperation: A.B. Dick Co., Addressograph-Multigraph Corp., Advance Process Supply Co., ATF Davidson Co., Brandtjen-Kluge Co., Brodhead Garrett Co., The Challenge Machinery Co., R.R. Donnelly & Sons Co., FORMATT Cut-out Acetate Art Aids, General Binding Corp., General Research Inc., Gravure Technical Association Inc., Hamilton Industries, Heidelberg Eastern, Inc., Hunt Manufacturing Co., IBM Office Products Division, Koh-I-Noor Rapidograph Inc., MBM Corp., Mergenthaler Linotype Co., Monotype International, NuArc Co. Inc., Joseph E. Podgor Co. Inc., Polaroid Corp., Rand McNally & Co., Rembrandt Graphics Arts, H.B. Rouse & Co., Scriptomatic Inc., Southern Gravure Service Inc., Strip Print Inc., Sun Chemical Co., Typographic Sales Inc., Vanderson Corp., and Zipatone Inc.

The Publisher

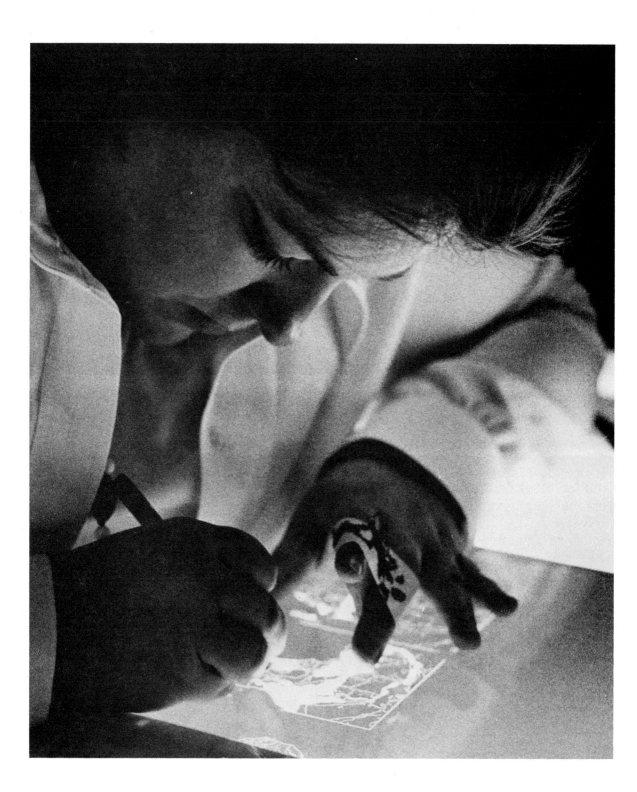

# THE GRAPHIC ARTS

1

People have always had a need to communicate. Primitive people communicated by grunting, laughing, frowning, and screaming. By these and other techniques they made their message clear to others.

As time went on, our ancestors developed other ways to communicate. They learned to mark trails with piles of stones. They learned to record events by painting pictures on cave walls. They learned to communicate through a spoken language. And they learned to write.

Writing made it possible to record information and to send messages over great distances. Writing also allowed people to transmit knowledge to future generations.

Communications improved with the invention of writing. But there were still problems to be solved. Ways had

to be found to reproduce many copies of a message. Materials to write with and print on had to be developed. And inks to put the message onto paper had to be made.

**Figure I-1:** Cave drawings provide evidence of early attempts at writing. Pictures were used to record the hunt.

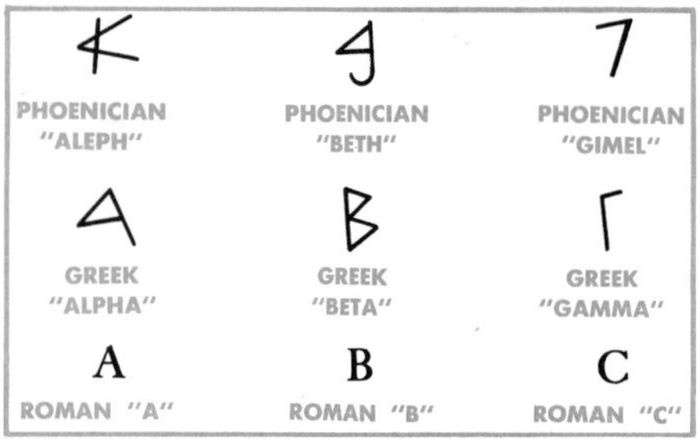

| | | |
|---|---|---|
| PHOENICIAN "ALEPH" | PHOENICIAN "BETH" | PHOENICIAN "GIMEL" |
| GREEK "ALPHA" | GREEK "BETA" | GREEK "GAMMA" |
| A | B | C |
| ROMAN "A" | ROMAN "B" | ROMAN "C" |

**Figure I-2:** How our alphabet evolved.

People solved each of these problems. They did so because they needed to communicate. And as they did, the graphic arts industry grew.

Our nation's graphic arts industry is the world's largest. It is comprised of more than 40,000 companies. Last year the industry employed over one million people.

When we think about an industry, we generally think in terms of the product it produces. The steel industry produces steel. The automotive industry produces automobiles. But what does the graphic arts industry produce?

The graphic arts industry produces *things that are printed.* Printed products are all around us. Some of these products are pictured in figure 1-1.

Most printed products carry a message. Printed messages are graphic or visual in form. They are made up of symbols, drawings, and photographs. Communication through the use of printed images is called <u>graphic communication</u>.

This book is a product of the graphic arts industry. Several individuals and business enterprises contributed to its creation. Together they represent the scope of the industry. So let's now look briefly at how this book was produced.

This book describes the tools, materials, and processes used by the graphic arts industry. It was written by the author after consultation with the publisher. The publisher provided editorial and design assistance. The publisher also managed the production of the book. After publication, the role of the publisher shifted to advertising and selling (figure 1-2).

**Figure 1-1:** A sampling of products produced by the graphic arts industry. (Sun Chemical Co.)

**Figure 1-2:** The publisher is generally involved in a book's development, production, and sale.

Type had to be set to form words contained within the book. A company that specializes in type composition provided this service (figure 1-3).

Artwork and photographs also had to be made. Artists created the illustrations. Photographers produced the photographs.

The assembled type, artwork, and photographs were then sent to a printer. The plates were made and the pages printed (figure 1-4).

From the printer the pages went to a bindery. At the bindery they were folded, sewn together, trimmed, and encased in a cover (figure 1-5).

The author, publisher, compositor, artist, photographer, printer, and binder all played important roles in the creation of this book. In addition, the

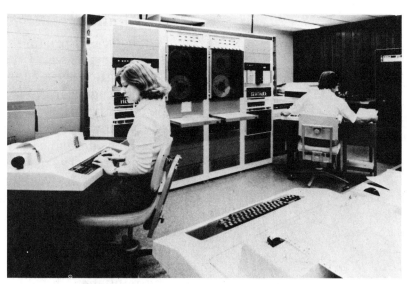

**Figure 1-3:** The compositor sets type to form words, sentences, and paragraphs. (Typographic Sales, Inc.)

products of paper and ink manufacturers were indispensible. It is clear that the scope of the industry encompasses a wide range of occupations, activities, and enterprises.

**Figure 1-4:** Multiple copies of the assembled type, artwork, and photographs are produced by the printer.

## SELF CHECK

1. List ten products that are produced by the graphic arts industry.
2. Explain the primary reason for producing newspapers, books, magazines, and other printed products.
3. List ten business enterprises and/or occupations that are part of the graphic arts industry.
4. What does the graphic arts industry produce?

**Figure 1-5:** The binder folds, sews, trims, and encloses the printed pages within a cover. (R. R. Donnelly & Sons Co.)

Choosing a career is an important decision. What do you want to do with your future? Perhaps the job for you is in the graphic arts.

The industry needs competent young men and women to fill a variety of jobs. Hundreds of different jobs exist. So how do you decide which one is for you?

Begin by looking at yourself as you are now. What are your interests? What do you like to do? What do you dislike doing? Where do your talents lie? Can you draw well? Are you a writer? Do you like working with people, or would you prefer to work with machines?

Then look to the future. How do you see yourself five or ten years from now? What are your goals? What do you want to do with your future?

Knowing yourself—your interests, your abilities, your desires—is the first step in choosing a career. The second step is to explore the job opportunities that are available.

Jobs in the graphic arts fall into eight categories. These categories are described below:

- Creative Professionals — Artist/designer, photographer, writer, reporter, and editor are some of the jobs in this category. People who hold these jobs create the

**Figure 2-1:** A commercial photographer preparing to shoot an assignment.

messages that are communicated graphically (figure 2-1).
- Craftspeople—A craft is an occupation requiring manual dexterity or specialized skills (figure 2-2). Workers who possess these skills are called craftspeople. Many craftspeople work in the graphic arts industry. Compositors, strippers, platemakers,

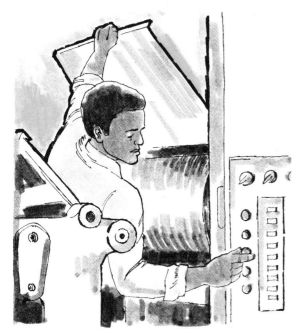

**Figure 2-2:** The operator of this offset press is a craftsperson.

process photographers, press operators, proofreaders, and bookbinders are some of the craftspeople employed by the industry.

**Figure 2-3:** A scientist at work. He is employed by a paper company to develop new products and new processes.

- Technologists—Scientists and engineers supply the industry with new ideas and inventions. Some are employed within the industry. Others work in related industries such as supply and equipment manufacturing (figure 2-3).
- Technicians—Included in this category are such jobs as quality control technician, estimator, and computer specialist. Each of these jobs require advanced technical training (figure 2-4).

- Marketers—Some salespeople demonstrate and sell equipment and supplies used within the industry. Others sell the products that the industry produces.
- Office and Clerical Workers —Secretaries, typists, and file clerks play an important role in the day-

**Figure 2-4:** This technician is testing ink to ensure its quality.

**Figure 2-5:** This person is operating an electronic typing system. The machine operates from magnetic tape or cards at speeds of up to 350 words a minute.

to-day operation of graphic arts firms. Secretaries take dictation, type letters, and answer phone calls. Typists may prepare letters and reports (figure 2-5). File clerks maintain the paperwork that is generated and received by the company.

● Managers and Owners—Managers and owners are the policy and decision-making men and women in the industry. Small business loans have helped many people start their own companies.

● Teachers—Teachers teach graphic arts courses in public and private schools (figure 2-6). Such courses may be part of an industrial arts, vocational, or technical education program. Instructors are also needed to provide training within the industry.

Are you interested in a career in the graphic arts? Talk it over with your parents. Discuss your plans with your guidance counselor and graphic arts teacher.

**Figure 2-6:** Teachers are needed to teach graphics arts in schools and industry.

Also talk to people who work in the graphic arts field. You can contact them through your local Printing Industries of America trade association, your local club of Printing House Craftsmen, and your local Litho Club. These are listed in the yellow pages of the telephone directory under "Associations".

Remember choosing a career is an important decision. Choose your job wisely!

## SELF CHECK

1. Explain why it is important to "know yourself" before choosing a career.
2. List the names of the eight general categories of jobs that exist in the graphic arts.
3. List three jobs in the graphic arts that you might consider undertaking as a career. Explain your reasons for selecting these jobs.
4. Describe how you would go about learning more about the jobs that exist in the graphic arts industry.

The proverb in figure 3-1 tells us that the best way to learn about graphic arts activities is by doing them. Projects are used for this purpose. Many graphic arts projects make use of machinery, and all machinery can be dangerous. At the same time that you are learning to do a project, you must also learn safe working habits by being safety conscious.

Three major dangers exist in every graphic arts shop:

- Chemicals
- Sharp tools
- Moving machinery

**Figure 3-2:** Shop safety is common sense. These ten rules will help you avoid injury.

I HEAR, I FORGET.
I SEE, I REMEMBER.
I DO, I UNDERSTAND.
—*Ancient Proverb*

**Figure 3-1:** Doing is learning.

Chemicals may stain skin or clothes, cause skin burns, injure the eyes, or poison the individual if swallowed.

Sharp tools may be as small as a mat knife or as large as an industrial paper cutter (figure 3-2). Both can seriously injure the careless worker or student.

Moving machinery may be the most dangerous shop equipment. It seems innocent until it snags a stray shirt cuff or wristwatch band. However small the machine is, it is usually stronger than the person trapped by it.

To prevent shop accidents, you should memorize the 10 simple rules listed in figure 3-3. Think about these rules so that you understand them.

- DO NOT ENTER THE SHOP UNLESS YOUR TEACHER IS IN THE ROOM.
- WEAR YOUR APRON. ROLL UP YOUR SLEEVES.
- REPORT UNSAFE CONDITIONS TO YOUR TEACHER IMMEDIATELY.
- DO NOT USE TOOLS OR MACHINES UNTIL YOU HAVE BEEN INSTRUCTED IN THEIR PROPER USE. DO NOT OPERATE EQUIPMENT WITHOUT YOUR TEACHER'S PERMISSION.
- CARRY SHARP TOOLS WITH THEIR CUTTING EDGES DOWN.
- DO NOT PUT DIRTY HANDS IN YOUR MOUTH. WASH YOUR HANDS BEFORE LEAVING THE SHOP.
- DO NOT LEAVE SCRAPS OR OTHER MATERIALS ON THE FLOOR. SOMEONE MIGHT SLIP AND FALL.
- BE CAREFUL WHEN PASSING TOOLS AND MATERIALS TO OTHERS IN THE CLASS.
- REPORT ALL ACCIDENTS TO YOUR TEACHER IMMEDIATELY. EVEN THE MINOR ONES SHOULD BE REPORTED.
- ALWAYS THINK BEFORE DOING!

**Figure 3-3:** Shop safety is common sense. These ten rules will help you avoid injury.

## SELF CHECK

1. What is the best way to understand the job you are learning?

2. What three dangers exist in every shop?
3. Name the 10 rules of safety.
4. List 5 graphic arts projects that you would like to make.

Type provides us with a way to make words into a printed message. There are two basic methods used to set or compose type.

- Hot-type composition
- Cold-type composition

Hot type is made from molten metal. Many copies of a message can be printed directly from hot type. Hand-set foundry type (figure 4-1) is considered hot type. Linotype slugs (figure 4-2) contain an entire line of symbols on a single body. They also fall into the hot type category.

**Figure 4-2:** A Linotype slug contains an entire line of symbols on a single body. Linotype is a hot-type composition method.

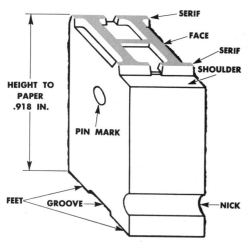

**Figure 4-1:** Foundry type is used for hot-type composition.

**Figure 4-3:** A preprinted alphabet used for cold-type composition. (Zipatone Inc.)

**Figure 4-4:** An IBM Selectric Composing typewriter used for cold-type composition. Typing elements (arrow) can be changed to provide different type faces. (IBM Office Products Division)

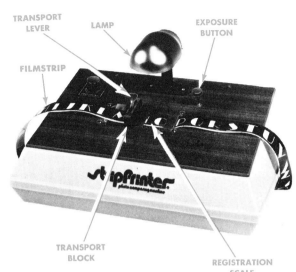

TRANSPORT LEVER    LAMP    EXPOSURE BUTTON

FILMSTRIP

TRANSPORT BLOCK    REGISTRATION SCALE

**Figure 4-5:** The StripPrinter. Symbols are generated on photographic paper by exposing the paper through a strip of plastic containing characters in negative form. (StripPrinter Inc.)

Cold type is made in three ways:

- Hand-assembling preprinted paper and plastic letters (figure 4-3)
- Using a typewriter (figure 4-4)
- Using photographic techniques (figure 4-5)

The term face refers to the printing surface of a piece of hot type or the shape of a cold type letter. There are many type faces available to the printer. Literally thousands of faces exist. Fortunately, all faces can be grouped into six major classes or styles.

- **Text type faces** (figure 4-6) are hard to read. Letter shapes resemble the hand-drawn letters of early scribes. They should never be composed using all capital letters. It would be almost impossible to read a message set in this manner.

Old English

American Text

Goudy Text

Cloister Text

Claudius

Fraktur

**Figure 4-6:** Common text type faces.

ABCDEFGHIJK
LMNOPQRSTU
VWXYZÆØ ab
cdefghijklmnop
qrstuvwxyzæø1
234567890&?!£
$(;)≈≂≈≙«»

OLDSTYLE

ABCDEFGHIJKL
MNOPQRSTUVW
XYZÆØ abcdefgg
hijk lmnopqrstuv
wxyyzæø 123456
7890&?!£$(;)——·≍«»≍

MODERN

ABCDEFGHIJK
LMNOPQRSTU
VWXYZÆØ ab
cdefghijklmnop
qrstuvw xyzæø
1234567890 &?!£
$(;)≂≈«()≍≍ ≂≡

TRANSITIONAL

**Figure 4-7:** The three styles of Roman type.

*Helvetica*

News Gothic

American Typewriter

ENGINEERING

Optima

Rockwell

Univers 55

**Horatio**

L&C Stymie Liteline

**Figure 4-8:** Sans serif type faces do not have serifs. There is little variation in the thickness of letterstrokes.

**City**

Bulletin

Lubalin Graph

**Figure 4-9:** Examples of square serif type faces.

● **Roman type faces** (figure 4-7) are easy to read. They are patterned after letters used in early Roman inscriptions. There are three different styles of Roman type: oldstyle, modern, and transitional. Each is characterized by the shape of its serifs and the thick and thin strokes that make up its symbols. <u>Serifs</u> are the short cross lines located at the ends of the main strokes.

● **Sans serif type faces** (figure 4-8) do not have serifs. There is little variation in the thickness and weight of letter strokes.

● **Square serif type faces** (figure 4-9) are geometric in design. The serifs at the end of the strokes are square. These faces are used mainly for headlines, advertisements, and short pieces of reading matter. They should not be used where large amounts of copy must be read.

- **Script type faces** (figure 4-10) resemble handwriting. They are hard to read, and should never be composed using all capital letters.
- **Novelty type faces** (figure 4-11) are also called *decorative* type. These faces are generally used to do two

*Commercial Script*

*Juliet*

**Brody**

*Murray Hill Bold*

*Palace Script*

**Brush Script**

**Figure 4-10:** Script type faces resemble handwriting.

GLASER STENCIL

**Shatter**

STRIPES

Octopuss

NEON

PIONEER

**Figure 4-11:** Novelty type faces can be used to get the receiver's attention and to establish a mood.

Futura Demi Bold Outline Shadow
ABCDEFGHIJKLMNOPQRSTUVWXYZ&.,;;!
¿'""()*- abcdefghijklmnopqrstuvwxyz/%$¢
1234567890$¢1234567890

**Figure 4-12:** A font of type includes capital and lowercase letters, numbers and punctuation marks of one size and style.

things: to get attention and to establish a mood.

Type is sold by the font. A <u>font</u> (figure 4-12) is a complete assortment of characters of one size and style. A font of type includes capital and lower-case letters, numbers, and punctuation marks.

The term <u>series</u> is used when referring to a type style available in several sizes. All of the available sizes of the font shown in figure 4-12 would be a type series.

A <u>family</u> (figure 4-13) is a group of related type faces. Each member of a type family has the same basic name. Members also have the same general design characteristics. They differ, however, in terms of the weight of the face, the amount of space allotted to each character, and the angle of each character.

Our system of measurement (inches and fractions of inches) is not used to measure type. It is too hard. Instead, a special system called the <u>point system</u> has been developed to measure type (figure 4-14).

The basic unit of the point system is the <u>point</u>. One point is equal to 1/72 inch. There are 72 points in one inch.

Twelve points equal one <u>pica</u>. Six picas equal one inch. A half of a pica (6

```
1 POINT = 1/72 INCH
1 INCH = 72 POINTS
12 POINTS = 1 PICA
6 PICAS = 1 INCH
6 POINTS (1/2 PICA) = 1 NONPAREIL
5 1/2 POINTS = 1 AGATE
```

**Figure 4-14:** The printer's point system of measurement.

Anyone responsive to the beauty of fine typography will appreciate the flexibility of spacing offered by the Alphatype. ABCDEFGHIJKLMNOPQRSTUVWXYZ12345
*Futura Book*

Anyone responsive to the beauty of fine typography will appreciate the flexibility of spacing offered by the Alphatype. ABCDEFGHIJKLMNOPQRSTUVWXYZ12345
*Futura Book Italic*

Anyone responsive to the beauty of fine typography will appreciate the flexibility of spacing offered by the Alphatype. ABCDEFGHIJKLMNOPQRSTUVWXYZ12345
*Futura Medium*

Anyone responsive to the beauty of fine typography will appreciate the flexibility of spacing offered by the Alphatype. ABCDEFGHIJKLMNOPQRSTUVWXYZ12345
*Futura Medium Italic*

**Anyone responsive to the beauty of fine typography will appreciate the flexibility of spacing offered by the Alphatype. ABCDEFGHIJKLMNOPQRSTUVWXYZ12345**
*Futura Demibold*

**Anyone responsive to the beauty of fine typography will appreciate the flexibility of spacing offered by the Alphatype. ABCDEFGHIJKLMNOPQRSTUVWXYZ12345**
*Futura Demibold Italic*

**Anyone responsive to the beauty of fine typography will appreciate flexibility of spacing offered by Alphatype. ABCDEFGHIJKLMNOPQRSTUVWXYZ**
*Futura Bold*

**Anyone responsive to the beauty of fine typography will appreciate flexibility of spacing offered by Alphatype. ABCDEFGHIJKLMNOPQRSTUVWXYZ**
*Futura Bold Italic*

**Figure 4-13:** A family is a group of related type faces.

**Figure 4-15:** A line gage is a printer's ruler.

# ABCDEefg
60 pt.

# ABCDEF fghij
48 pt.

## ABCDEfghijk
36 pt.

### ABCDEFGhijklmn
24 pt.

#### ABCDEFGHIJklmnopqrs
18 pt.

**Figure 4-16:** The face on a piece of foundry type is always smaller than the type body.

points) is called a <u>nonpareil</u>. There are 12 nonpareils in an inch.

A line gage (figure 4-15) is a printer's ruler. It is used to determine point and pica measurement. Note that it contains two scales, an inch scale and a pica scale.

Type is measured in points. Other sizes are available, but the most common sizes of type range from 6 through 72 points.

The body of a piece of hot type determines its size designation. The relationship between type body and type face is shown in figure 4-16.

Cold type size is determined by measuring from the top of a tall <u>ascender</u> letter to the bottom of a <u>descender</u> letter. Ascender letters are b, d, f, h, k, l, and t. Descender letters are g, j, p, and q.

---

**SELF CHECK**

1. Describe the difference between hot-type composition and cold-type composition.
2. Using newspapers and old magazines as a source, locate an example of each of the 6 major classes or styles of type. Label each type style.
3. Describe the relationship among the units of measurement in the printer's point system.
4. Define the terms: type font, type series, and type family.

In simple terms, two kinds of pictures are used in the graphic arts. They are:

- Drawings
- Photographs

Drawings are created to add clarity or interest to a printed message. A line drawing is a drawing made of nothing but black lines. There are no shades of grey in a line drawing. Drawings can be divided into two general types:

- Pictorial drawings
- Technical drawings

Pictorial drawings (figure 5-1) are prepared by artists using freehand techniques. They are created on white paper with black ink. Specialized drawing instruments are not generally needed.

Use a good quality white paper or board. Avoid the use of uncoated papers. They tend to absorb the ink and give a ragged edge to the inked line.

Use light-blue pencils to make guidelines. Press lightly on the pencil. Guidelines prepared in this manner do not have to be erased. When photographed, light-blue lines are seen by the film as though they were white.

Use inking pens and felt-tip pens to draw black lines. Pencil images should be avoided because they do not photograph well. Small paint brushes and black drawing ink can be used to fill in large areas or create special effects. A set of interchangeable quill

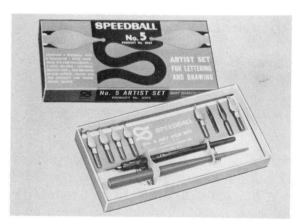

**Figure 5-2:** A set of interchangeable quill points used for freehand lettering and sketching. (Hunt Manufacturing Co.)

**Figure 5-1:** A pictorial drawing. It was prepared by an artist using freehand techniques.

**Figure 5-3:** This ruling pen comes with interchangeable points for controlling line width. (Koh-I-Noor Rapidograph, Inc.)

**Figure 5-5:** A page from a clip art book.

points used for freehand lettering and sketching is shown in figure 5-2. A ruling pen with interchangeable points for controlling line width is pictured in figure 5-3.

Drafters develop <u>technical drawings</u> (figure 5-4) with the aid of drawing instruments. These drawings are often used to show parts and assemblies

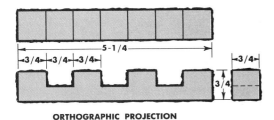

**ORTHOGRAPHIC PROJECTION**

**ISOMETRIC PROJECTION**

**Figure 5-4:** Technical drawings are often included in service and operation manuals to show parts and assemblies.

described in service and operation manuals.

It is not always necessary to create drawings from scratch. Often, preprinted <u>clip art</u> (figure 5-5) can be used.

Clip art is available in sheet and book formats. Each sheet or book page contains several black and white illustrations in a variety of sizes. The purchase price generally includes permission to reproduce the illustrations.

Like drawings, <u>photographs</u> are used to add clarity or interest to a printed message. They are made with a camera

**Figure 5-6:** Photographic messages are much like spoken or written ones. What is the subject of this photograph? What is its predicate? (Polaroid Corp.)

A photographic statement is like a spoken or written one. All three have subject elements and predicate elements. The <u>subject</u> is the main element in the photograph. It is what the photograph is about. The <u>predicate element</u> tells us something about the subject. It shows us what the subject is doing.

Photographs for reproduction can be purchased from professional sources. Sometimes they can be obtained at no cost from industrial concerns and advertising agencies. Most often, however, a photograph having the desired subject and predicate will have to be taken.

and are a light image of an actual object or scene (figure 5-6). A drawing shows only what is desired, but a photograph usually shows more.

| SELF CHECK |
| --- |

1. Explain the difference between pictorial and technical drawings.
2. Define "clip art".
3. Describe what is meant by the term "photographic statement".
4. Identify the subject and predicate elements of the photograph shown in figure 5-6.

The key element in all graphic arts is planning. Usually planning is done by a designer or editor who attempts to answer certain questions which his or her design will satisfy. The basic questions are:

- What is the message?
- For whom is the message intended?
- How will the message be sent?

It is important to know what the message is. Sometimes companies design advertisements that win prizes for beauty, but forget to sell the product. A design can be very pretty, but it is worthless if the message is left out (figure 6-1).

The person for whom the message is intended must be able to understand it. If the receiver of the message can't read, or doesn't read well, the message shouldn't use many words (figure 6-2).

How the message is to be sent determines what form it will take. Is it going to be a billboard, a magazine, or even a letter? Billboards use big pictures and words that can be read from a distance. Magazines use typography (type) and pictures to get the reader's attention. Letters depend on the arrangement of the information to hold the reader's interest.

**Figure 6-1:** A design can be worthless if the message is left out. In the illustration on the left, only half the message is in the advertisement. The ad won't work. On the right, the telephone number has been added. That's the message.

**Figure 6-2:** The person who reads the message is important. In this sample, one design says "call today", the other design has more words. If the person who reads it is in a hurry, which is the best design?

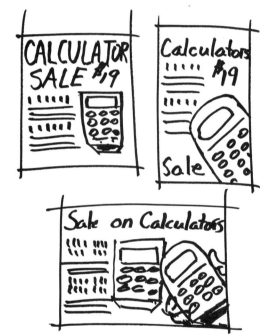

- WHAT IS THE MESSAGE TO BE TRANSMITTED?
- WHY IS IT BEING TRANSMITTED?
- DOES THE TYPE OF MESSAGE NECESSITATE A PARTICULAR KIND OF TREATMENT? FOR EXAMPLE, MUST IT BE DIGNIFIED OR CAN IT BE HUMOROUS?
- HOW WILL THE FINISHED PRODUCT BE USED?
- WHAT AUDIENCE DO YOU WISH TO REACH?
- WHAT FORM WILL THE PRODUCT TAKE?
- WILL IT BE A SINGLE SHEET, A BOOKLET, AN ENTIRE BOOK?
- ARE ILLUSTRATIONS TO BE USED? WILL THEY BE DRAWINGS, PHOTOGRAPHS, OR A COMBINATION OF BOTH?
- WHAT SIZE WILL THE FINISHED PRODUCT BE?
- WILL THE SHEETS BE TRIMMED, FOLDED, PERFORATED?
- WILL THE SHEETS BE BOUND? HOW?
- BY WHAT METHOD WILL THE PRODUCT BE PRINTED?
- WHAT TYPE OF PAPER WILL BE USED? WHAT ABOUT THE COLOR OF THE PAPER?
- WILL COLORED INKS BE USED? WHICH COLORS?
- HOW MANY COPIES WILL BE PRINTED? WILL REPRINTS BE NEEDED?
- HOW LONG WILL IT TAKE TO COMPLETE THE JOB?
- HOW MUCH WILL IT COST?

**Figure 6-3:** When you know the answers to these questions you are ready to begin a layout.

**Figure 6-4:** Thumbnail sketches are used to explore and develop ideas.

Information is needed in order to plan effectively. One way to obtain this information is to ask questions. Ask questions of yourself and others involved in producing the printed product. Some questions that should be asked are shown in figure 6-3.

After these questions have been answered, the next step is to develop a graphic plan for the printed product. This plan is called a <u>layout</u>.

A layout reflects the visual appearance of a job to be printed. It shows the arrangement of type, illustrations, and ornamentation. It need not, and generally does not, contain the actual elements to be included in the final product. Symbols are often used to represent these elements.

There are three types of layouts. They are:

- Thumbnail sketch
- Rough layout
- Comprehensive layout

Thumbnail sketches (figure 6-4) are used to explore and develop ideas. These sketches are done rapidly. They present overall design features rather than design details. They are usually prepared in a reduced size.

The rough layout (figure 6-5) is used to show space relationships among all of the elements in a printed job. A rough layout is made by refining the best of the thumbnail sketches.

The rough layout is drawn.to the same size as the finished job. It contains more detail than the thumbnail. Large size type is "roughed in". Small type is denoted by drawing parallel lines. The content of pictures is suggested and their positions are shown.

The comprehensive layout (figure 6-6) is a prototype of the proposed product. It should come as close to

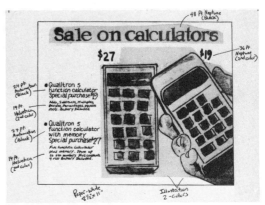

**Figure 6-6:** The comprehensive layout is a prototype of the proposed product. It serves as a guide or blueprint to those who produce the printed item.

duplicating the final product as possible, even though the actual type and illustrations have not yet been generated.

The comprehensive layout allows everyone involved with the product to see it before it is printed. It provides an opportunity to make final changes. And it serves as a guide or blueprint to those who produce the printed item.

**Figure 6-5:** The rough layout is used to show space relationships among all of the elements in a printed job.

## SELF CHECK

1. List and describe the characteristics of a thumbnail sketch.
2. List and describe the characteristics of a rough layout.
3. List and describe the characteristics of a comprehensive layout.
4. Prepare a rough layout for a one page, 8½" x 11" flyer, that will be used to advertise a product of your

# 2 LETTERPRESS PRINTING

Printing from a raised surface is called letterpress printing. Letterpress is the oldest printing method. It was first used by the Chinese around 770 A.D. They made many copies of a picture from a single wooden plate. Relief printing is another name for letterpress printing.

When ink is applied to a raised surface and paper is pressed against the inked surface, the ink will be transferred to the paper (figure II-1). Relief or letterpress are terms used to describe printing methods that use this principle. The rubber stamp shown in figure II-2 is a letterpress printing device. It transfers ink from a raised surface to paper. The typewriter element shown in figure II-3 also prints in this way.

Foundry type, Monotype, Linotype, and Ludlow (figure II-4) are used by the letterpress printer to transfer information to paper. The plates shown in figure II-5 are also used in letterpress

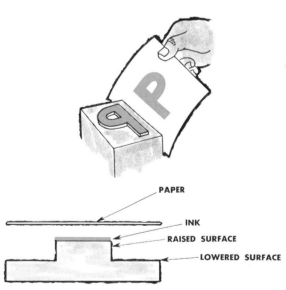

**Figure II-1:** Relief or letterpress printing. The lowered surface does not print because it doesn't come in contact with the ink or the paper.

**Figure II-2:** Printing with a rubber stamp is a form of letterpress printing.

**Figure II-3:** Relief printing elements are used in typewriters. (IBM Office Products Division).

printing; their raised surfaces can print photographs and line illustrations as well as letters and numbers.

The principle of printing from a raised surface is not very hard to understand. However, there is one problem we must consider. Look at figure II-1 again. Note the shape of the raised surface that printed the letter

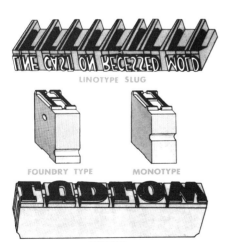

**Figure II-4:** Foundry type, Monotype, Linotype, and Ludlow.

"P". It is backwards, or "wrong reading". The raised surface was made this way so it would print a "right reading" image on the paper. The reason for reversing the image on a letterpress plate is illustrated in figure II-6.

WOOD ENGRAVING

LINOLEUM BLOCK

PHOTOENGRAVING

WOOD CUT

**Figure II-5:** Letterpress plates include linoleum blocks, wood cuts, wood engravings, and photoengravings.

**Figure II-6:** The raised surface of a letterpress plate must be prepared in reverse. The symbols or characters on this type of plate are "wrong reading" or a mirror image of what is to be printed. Hold this page up to a mirror to find out what this plate will print.

Foundry type and wood type are both set by hand. Individual characters are taken from a type case and set or assembled in a composing stick to form words, sentences, and paragraphs.

There are two kinds of hand-set type:

- Foundry type
- Wood type

Foundry type (figure 7-1) is made from an alloy of lead, antimony and tin. The greatest percentage of metal in the alloy is lead.

Each piece of foundry type measures exactly .918 of an inch long. At one end

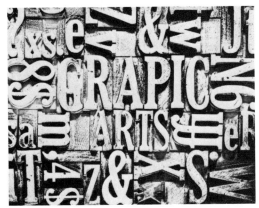

**Figure 7-2:** Wood type faces are carved in the end grain of specially treated hardwoods.

is a raised character. The face of the character carries the ink and is a mirror image of the symbol to be printed.

Wood type (figure 7-2) is generally used for poster printing. Characters are large and are carved into the end grain of specially treated hardwoods. Wood type is much lighter in weight than metal type of the same size.

Hand-set type is stored in shallow drawers called cases. The California job case (figure 7-3) is the most often used arrangement for storing type. It has 89 compartments for separating pieces of type. Because of the difference in size of type letters and their frequency of use, the compartments in a type case vary in size. There are fewer q's, x's, and z's in a case because they aren't needed. But h's and e's are

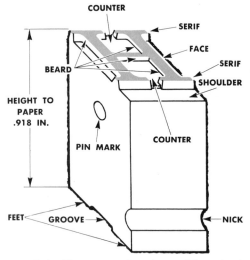

**Figure 7-1:** The parts of a piece of foundry type. Foundry type is made from an alloy of lead, antimony, and tin. It melts at 850°F and is always .918 inch long.

| ffi | fl | 5-EM | 4-EM | ' | k | | 1 | 2 | 3 | 4 | 5 | 6 | 7 | 8 | | $ | | | Æ | Œ | æ | œ |
|---|---|---|---|---|---|---|---|---|---|---|---|---|---|---|---|---|---|---|---|---|---|---|
| j | b | c | d | e | | | i | s | f | g | ff | 9 | | | A | B | C | D | E | F | G |
| ? | | | | | | | | | | | fi | 0 | | | | | | | | | |
| ! | l | m | n | h | | | o | y | p | w | , | EN QUADS | EM QUADS | | H | I | K | L | M | N | O |
| z | | | | | | | | | | | | | | | | | | | | | |
| x | v | u | t | 3-EM SPACES | | a | r | ; | : | 2-EM AND 3-M QUADS | | | P | Q | R | S | T | V | W |
| q | | | | | | | | | . | - | | | | X | Y | Z | J | U | & | ffl |

**Figure 7-3:** Hand-set type is stored in type cases. The most commonly used type case arrangement is the California job case. However, there are other arrangements.

used a lot in making words, so there is more space for them.

Uppercase or capital letters are stored in the compartments located on the right-hand side of the case. With two exceptions, they are arranged in alphabetical order. Capital J's and Capital U's follow the Z.

Lowercase or small letters are stored in compartments located in the left and center sections of the case. The letters used the most are stored in the larger, more centrally located compartments.

Type faces are cast in reverse. Because of this, some letters are difficult to distinguish. They look like other letters. Letters that are difficult to distinguish are called demons (figure 7-4).

The apostrophe is located to the left of the lowercase k in the left-hand

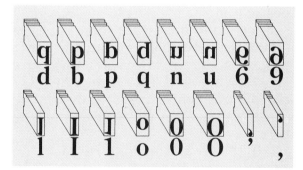

**Figure 7-4:** Demon type characters, and how they appear when printed.

third of the case. Commas, semicolons, colons, periods, and hyphens are located in the center section of the case.

The numbers 0 through 9 are located in compartments at the top of the

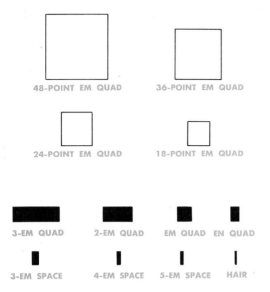

**Figure 7-5:** Different sizes of em quads. An em is equal in size to the square of the type body.

**Figure 7-6:** The relationship among spaces, en, and em quads.

center section of the case. Individual numbers can be combined to form any desired number.

Spaces and quads are pieces of type metal that are shorter than the other pieces of type. Because they are shorter they will not print when the assembled type is inked and printed. Instead they form white spaces on the printed copy.

All spaces and quads are based on the em, which is equal in measurement to the square of the type body size in the case (figure 7-5). The relationship among spaces, en, and em quads is shown in figure 7-6.

A ligature is a single type body with two or more letters forming the face. Ligatures are included with some italic types to prevent letters, that overhang their body, from breaking. The common ligatures are; fi, ff, fl, ffi, and ffl.

Diphthongs consist of two joined vowels on one body. Diphthongs are included with some styles of type to improve the appearance of the printed product. The common diphthongs are Æ, Œ, æ, and œ.

---

**SELF CHECK**

1. Sketch a piece of foundry type and label its parts.
2. Refer to figure 7-3 and locate in alphabetical order each uppercase letter and each lowercase letter. Then note the location of punctuation marks, figures, spaces, and quads.
3. Using simple diagrams, illustrate the relationship among the various spaces and quads found in a California job case.
4. What is a demon?

Hand-setting of letterpress type was once a skill every typographer had to do well. Even today, you should know how to do it. Hand-set type may be disappearing from many type shops, but it still has its specialized uses.

There are two ways to set letterpress type:

- Hand composition
- Machine composition

Hand composition is done in a composing stick. The composing stick (figure 8-1) is used to hold the type while it is being set into words and sentences. The stick is adjustable in pica graduations.

Thin strips of type metal are used to provide space between the lines of type in the stick. These strips of metal do not print and are called leads and slugs. A lead is generally 1 or 2 points thick and may be cut to any desired length. A slug is usually 6 points thick. It also can be cut to any length desired. A lead and slug cutter (figure 8-2) is

**Figure 8-2:** Lead and slug cutter. (Brodhead-Garrett Co.)

**Figure 8-3:** Hand miterer. (H. B. Rouse & Co.)

used to cut leads and slugs to length.

Strips of type-high metal (.918 inch) are used to print straight lines of various thicknesses. Such strips are called rules and are made from brass or type metal. A lead and slug cutter is also used to cut rules to length.

Borders are pieces of type or strips of type-high metal used to provide decoration within or around a type form. A hand miterer (figure 8-3) is used to miter the corners of border strips when it is necessary to completely surround the type form.

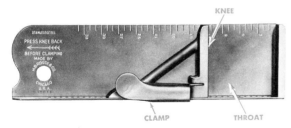

**Figure 8-1:** Parts of a composing stick. (Brodhead-Garrett Co.)

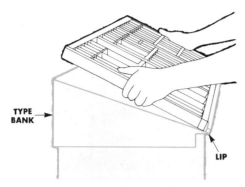

**Figure 8-4:** Be sure to position the case behind the lip of the slanted top. Otherwise it may slide to the floor.

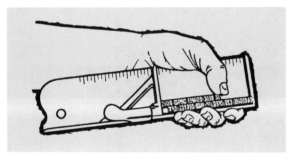

**Figure 8-5:** How to hold a composing stick. Type is laid in the composing stick from left to right.

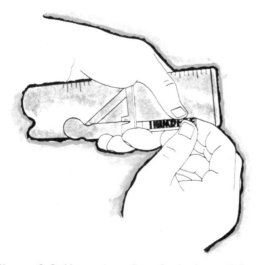

**Figure 8-6:** How a type form looks in a stick.

The hand-setting of foundry type begins by carefully removing the case from the type bank (cabinet) and placing it on top of the bank (figure 8-4). Be sure to position the case behind the lip of the slanted top. The lip prevents the case from sliding to the floor.

Adjust the composing stick to the desired line length or measure for the job. Lock the knee in position before proceeding.

Cut a slug to length on the lead and slug cutter and place it in the stick. To prevent binding, the slug should be cut slightly shorter than the measure (width) of the job.

Foundry type is set by removing individual characters from the job case and placing them into the composing stick. Hold the stick in the left hand as shown in figure 8-5. The right hand is used to pick up the type from the case and transfer it to the composing stick.

Type is set from left to right. Always start at the knee of the stick and work toward the solid end. The nick on each piece of type must face up toward the open side of the composing stick (figure 8-6).

The usual ways of setting type are:

- Flush left
- Flush right
- Centered
- Justified

To set type flush left, begin by inserting the first letter of the first word next to the knee of the stick. The nick must face up toward the open side. Repeat this process until the first word has been set. Insert a 3-em space and set the next word. Continue this process until all of the words that appear in the first line are completed.

Use quads and spaces to fill or "quad out" the line. Small spaces should be placed next to the last word. Large spaces or quads are used to end the line. This will prevent the small spaces from falling when the type is removed from the stick.

By trying various combinations of spaces and quads, line length can be accurately controlled. It should never be necessary to force a space of quad into the composing stick. A properly set line is one that can stand alone in the stick when the entire line is tilted forward.

After the first line is completed, insert a lead or slug. Repeat the above procedure when setting the second line of type. Continue this process until the stick is full or until all of the required type has been set (figure 8-7).

The procedures for setting type <u>flush right</u> (figure 8-8) are similar to those used when setting type flush left. There are two basic differences, however. First, after the words have been set and before the line is quaded out, the entire line of type is pushed away from the knee and moved toward the solid side of the stick. The second difference is that spaces and quads are added at the beginning rather than at the end of each line of type.

The procedures for setting type <u>on center</u> (figure 8-9), are similar to those used for setting type flush left. This time, however, the lines are centered within the composing stick by placing an equal number of spacing units at the beginning and end of each line. Spaces

This copy is set flush left.
All lines start at the left margin.
Quads and spaces are used to
fill out each line.

**Figure 8-7:** Type set flush with the left-hand margin.

This copy is set flush right.
All lines end at the right margin.
Spaces and quads are added at
the beginning of each line of type.

**Figure 8-8:** Type set flush with the right-hand margin.

This copy is set on center.
Place an equal number of spaces
and quads at the beginning
and end of each line.

**Figure 8-9:** Type set on center.

This copy is justified. Justification is
accomplished by adjusting the spaces
used between words. All lines of
type are exactly the same length.

**Figure 8-10:** Justified type.

**Figure 8-11:** Linotype typesetting machine. (Mergenthaler Linotype Co.)

**Figure 8-12:** A Linotype slug.

then stored in California job cases. Typesetting machines do not store type. They store molds used to make type. Typesetting machines cast and set their own type. This type is generally melted down and the type metal reused after the form has been printed.

Other machines, such as the Linotype (figure 8-11) and Intertype produce a complete line of characters, all cast on a single body. These lines of type are called slugs (figure 8-12).

and quads used at the end of a line must match the spaces and quads placed at the beginning.

Justification (figure 8-10) is accomplished by adjusting the size of the spaces used between words so that all lines of type are exactly the same length.

Sometimes a complete word cannot be included in a single line, even after adjusting the spaces between words in that line. When necessary, such words can be hyphenated. The word is divided in two. The first part of the word, followed by a hyphen, ends the original line. The second part of the same word starts the next line. The place or places where a word may be hyphenated can be found in a dictionary.

Hand-set type is cast in a foundry

| | SELF CHECK |
|---|---|

1. Name the two most common types of hand-set type.
2. Explain the meaning of flush left, flush right, centered, and justified type.
3. Why is machine-set type different from hand-set type?
4. Using X's to represent type characters and O's to represent spacing materials, draw three lines of type flush left, three lines flush right, three lines on center, and three justified lines. Base your illustrations on a line length of 3 inches (18 picas).

The image carriers or plates used in letterpress printing are called letterpress plates. There are two basic types of letterpress plates:

- Original plates
- Duplicate plates

Original plates for letterpress printing are made with hand-set or machine-set hot type. They may also be made by hand-cutting linoleum or wood blocks. Letterpress plates produced through photographic techniques (photoengravings) are also called original plates.

Linoleum and wood plates are made by carving on the flat surface of a linoleum or wood block. Areas that do not print must be cut away. The image to be printed is left raised on the surface of the block. Linoleum is easier to cut than wood.

To prepare a linoleum block, begin by choosing a design to be reproduced. Your first design should consist of solid areas of a single color with lots of heavy lines like the one shown in figure 9-1. Avoid designs with fine lines. They are difficult to cut and can collapse or break during the printing process.

Next, the design must be transferred (in reverse) to the surface of the block (figure 9-2). Carbon paper may be used for this purpose. Place the carbon

**Figure 9-1:** A design suitable for linoleum block printing. It consists of heavy lines and solid areas of color.

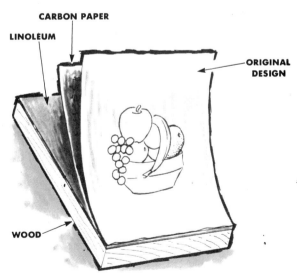

**Figure 9-2:** Transferring the design onto a linoleum block.

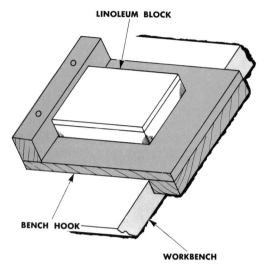

LINOLEUM BLOCK

BENCH HOOK

WORKBENCH

**Figure 9-3:** Use a bench hook to hold the linoleum block while it is being cut.

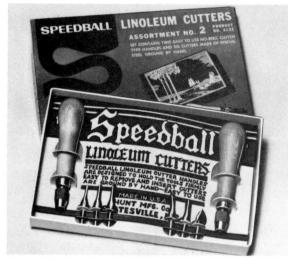

**Figure 9-4:** Linoleum block carving tools. (Hunt Manufacturing Co.)

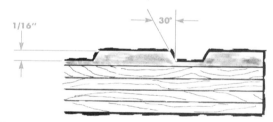

1/16"   30°

**Figure 9-5:** Avoid undercutting the image areas. Outline cuts should be made at a 30° angle to the printing surface.

paper, carbon side down, on the surface of the block. Place the design on the back of the carbon paper. The backside of the paper containing the design should face up. Use tape to hold the carbon paper and design in position on the block. By tracing over the back of the original design the image will transfer in reverse onto the surface of the linoleum. Use india ink and a pen to ink the carbon image that has been placed on the block. This is done so the image will remain on the block without smudging while you carve it.

A bench hook (figure 9-3) holds the block while it is being carved.

A set of linoleum block carving tools (figure 9-4) consists of a single handle and several cutting tools. Three basic types of cutting tools are included. These are the knife, the veiner, and the gouge.

Both the knife and veiner can be used to outline the image (figure 9-5). If a knife is used, hold it at a slight angle to avoid undercutting the raised image. The veiner, which is a V-shaped chisel, will automatically produce a beveled edge around the image. The point of the V must contact the linoleum throughout the cutting operation.

After the image is outlined, remove all non-image areas with a gouge. A

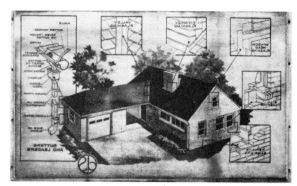

**Figure 9-6:** A photoengraving is an original letterpress plate.

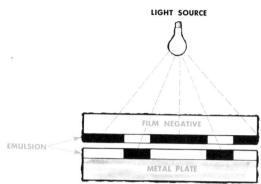

**Figure 9-7:** Exposing the photoengraving. Light passing through the transparent areas of the negative hardens the emulsion on the plate below. Because no light passes through the opaque areas of the negative, the emulsion below is not affected.

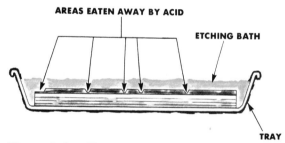

**Figure 9-8:** The areas under the resist are not eaten away by the etching bath.

gouge is a U-shaped chisel. All nonprinting areas must be cut at least 1/16 inch deep. Otherwise they may reproduce when the block is printed.

**Caution!** Linoleum carving tools are sharp. Handle them with care. Always push the cutting tool away from your body. Keep both hands behind the blade while cutting the linoleum block.

A separate block must be carved for each color in the design. If a two-color image is to be printed, two blocks must be carved. A four-color design requires four linoleum blocks.

Photoengravings (figure 9-6) are made by photographically transferring an image to metal or plastic plates coated with light-sensitive chemicals (figure 9-7).

After exposure the plate is processed. Processing makes the image visible and removes the light-sensitive coating from the unexposed areas of the plate.

The emulsion remaining on the plate after it is processed serves as a resist.

Areas beneath the resist are not affected when the plate is in an etching bath. The unprotected areas, however, are eaten away (figure 9-8).

Photoengravings can also be used to print photographs containing several shades of grey. Prints made from such

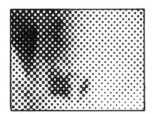

Figure 9-9: A halftone print. The size and spacing of the black dots creates the illusion of various tones of grey.

**Figure 9-10:** A stereotype matrix is needed to produce a stereotype plate.

plates are called halftones. By looking closely at a halftone, you can see that the inked areas are made of tiny dots instead of solid lines (figure 9-9). These These dots are so small that they are hard to see with the naked eye. When they are large and close together, they look black. When they are small and far apart they look white. Shades of grey depend on dot spacing and size.

Duplicate plates are letterpress plates made from molds taken from an original plate. Stereotypes, electrotypes, and rubber plates are examples of duplicate letterpress plates.

Stereotype plates are made by pressing the relief image from an original letterpress plate into a paper matrix (mold) (figure 9-10). Then molten metal is poured into the matrix in a casting box. When it hardens, the metal becomes a duplicate letterpress plate which can be used for printing.

Stereotype plates cannot be used to reproduce fine detail. The quality of a stereotype image is relatively poor. Stereotype plates are most often used for newspaper printing.

Electrotypes are high quality duplicate plates. Books and magazines produced by letterpress are generally printed from electrotype plates.

Electrotypes are produced by depositing or plating metal on molds made from original type forms and photoengravings. A special sheet of matrix material is placed over the type

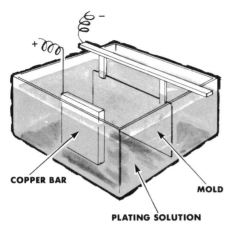

**COPPER BAR**

**MOLD**

**PLATING SOLUTION**

**Figure 9-11:** The electroplating process. The mold is connected to the negative terminal of a power source. A pure copper bar is attached to the positive terminal of the same power source. Both the mold and copper bar are suspended in a liquid plating solution. As current flows through the solution, copper atoms travel from the bar to the mold.

and photoengravings. After pressure has been applied to the matrix material, it is stripped from the original plate. The mold is then sprayed with silver paint so that it will conduct electricity during the plating operation.

The electroplating process is illustrated in figure 9-11. Plating is allowed to continue until a thin shell of copper is formed on the mold. Once formed,

the shell is removed from the mold and its back filled with a molten metal. After the metal solidifies, the electrotype is prepared for printing.

Rubber plates are also produced from molds. They are duplicate plates made from original type forms and photoengravings.

Most printing on paper, cellophane, and plastic bags is done from rubber plates using special inks. This process of printing is called flexography. A single flexible rubber plate is capable of a million or more printing impressions.

Rubber stamps are produced in much the same manner as are flexographic plates. The procedures for making rubber stamps are described in Unit 13.

## SELF CHECK

1. List the basic steps involved in preparing a linoleum block.
2. Identify the safety precautions to be taken when cutting a linoleum block.
3. Describe the major difference between original and duplicate letterpress plates.
4. Define the following terms: photoengravings, stereotypes, electrotypes, rubber plates.

A proof press (figure 10-1) is used to make the first print of a type form or linoleum block. This first print is called a <u>proof</u>. Making a proof is called <u>pulling a proof</u>. Proofs are pulled to check for errors before the job goes to press.

After the necessary lines of type have been set, the type is removed from the stick and tied with string. Removing the type form from the composing stick is called <u>dumping</u>.

Place the composing stick in a three-sided metal tray called a <u>galley</u>. Grasp

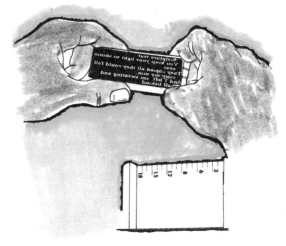

**Figure 10-2:** How to remove type from the composing stick.

**Figure 10-1:** Proofs of a type form or linoleum block are pulled on a proof press. (Challenge Machinery Co.)

the type form as shown in figure 10-2 and slide it out of the stick. Carefully move the type to a corner of the galley so that two of its sides are supported by two sides of the galley.

Tie a knot at one end of a piece of string long enough to wrap around the type form five or six times. Hold the knotted end of the string in your left hand. Position this end of the string at the upper left-hand corner of the form. Wind the string with your right hand in a clockwise direction around the form. Each time you come to the knot cross over it. Overlapping the knot in this way helps to bind the string in

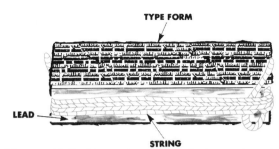

**Figure 10-3:** Use a lead to tuck the end of the string under the layers of string that are wrapped around the type form.

**Figure 10-5:** Inking a type form with a brayer.

position. Continue to wind the string around the form. Secure the end of the string by tucking it under the other layers of string (figure 10-3). Use a lead or piece of rule for this purpose.

Linoleum blocks must be made type-high before proofing. A type-high gage (figure 10-4) is used to determine the amount of chip board and paper that must be glued to the back of the block to make it .918 inches high.

Proofing is done in a galley on the proof press. To pull a proof place the galley on the bed of the proof press. The open end of the galley should face the cylinder. Carefully apply ink to the type face. A brayer (inking roller) is

used for this purpose. The procedure is as follows: place a small amount of ink on the ink plate. Run the brayer over the ink plate several times. Place the inked brayer on the type form and pass it lightly over the form (figure 10-5). Make sure that all areas of the form are inked.

Next place a clean sheet of paper on the inked form. Be careful not to move this paper once it contacts the form. Now roll the cylinder over the form. The pressure will cause the ink to transfer to the paper. Carefully strip this paper from the form as shown in figure 10-6. The proof should be sharp and legible. It is necessary to turn the open end of the galley toward the

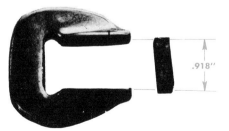

**Figure 10-4:** Use a type-high gage to check the height of the block. Type-high is .918 inch.

**Figure 10-6:** To avoid smudging use care when stripping the proof from the type form.

**Figure 10-7:** Wash the type form after proofing. Be sure to place all rags containing solvents in a special metal safety can.

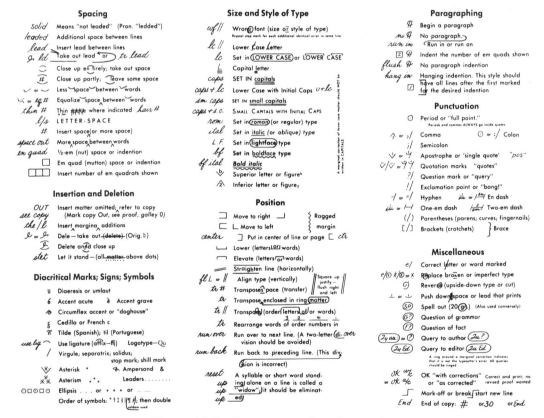

### Spacing

| | |
|---|---|
| *solid* | Means "not leaded" (Pron. "ledded") |
| *leaded* | Additional space between lines |
| *lead* | Insert lead between lines |
| *In ld* | take out lead or *tr lead* |
| ◡ | Close up entirely; take out space |
| # | Close up partly; leave some space |
| ◡ or ∨ | Less space between words |
| ◡ or *eg #* | Equalize space between words |
| *thin #* | Thin space where indicated *hair #* |
| *l/s* | LETTER-SPACE |
| # | Insert space (or more space) |
| *space out* | More space between words |
| *em quad* | ½-em (nut) space or indention |
| ▯ | Em quad (mutton) space or indention |
| ▯▯▯ | Insert number of em quadrats shown |

### Insertion and Deletion

| | |
|---|---|
| *OUT* | Insert matter omitted; refer to copy |
| *see copy* | (Mark copy Out, see proof, galley 0) |
| *the /l* | Insert margin additions |
| *l or l* | Dele — take out (delete) (Orig. b ) |
| ℐ | Delete and close up |
| *stet* | Let it stand — (all matter above dots) |

### Diacritical Marks; Signs; Symbols

| | |
|---|---|
| ◡ | Diaeresis or umlaut |
| ´ | Accent acute   ` Accent grave |
| ^ | Circumflex accent or "doghouse" |
| ¸ | Cedilla or French c |
| ˜ | Tilde (Spanish); til (Portuguese) |
| *use lig* ⁀ | Use ligature (affix ﬁ)   Logotype—Qu |
| / | Virgule; separatrix; solidus; stop mark; shill mark |
| ⚹ | Asterisk *   & Ampersand & |
| ⚹⚹ | Asterism *.*   Leaders . . . . . . . . |
| ○○○○○ | Ellipsis . . . or • • • or ... |
| | Order of symbols: * † ‡ § ‖ ¶ #; then double |

### Size and Style of Type

| | |
|---|---|
| *wf* ‖ | Wrong font (size or style of type) |
| | Repeat stop mark for each additional identical error in same line |
| *lc* ‖ | Lower case Letter |
| *lc* | Set in LOWER CASE or LOWER CASE |
| L | Capital letter |
| *caps* | SET IN capitals |
| *caps + lc* | Lower Case with Initial Caps *u+lc* |
| *sm. caps* | SET IN small capitals |
| *caps + s.c.* | SMALL CAPITALS WITH INITIAL CAPS |
| *rom.* | Set in roman (or regular) type |
| *ital* | Set in italic (or oblique) type |
| *L.F.* | Set in lightface type |
| *bf* | Set in boldface type |
| *bf ital* | Bold italic |
| ∨ | Superior letter or figure b |
| ∧ | Inferior letter or figure₂ |

### Position

| | |
|---|---|
| ⊐ | Move to right ⊐   Ragged |
| ⊏ | Move to left ⊏   margin |
| *center* | Put in center of line or page ⊏ *ctr* |
| ⊔ | Lower (letters or words) |
| ⊓ | Elevate (letters or words) |
| | Straighten line (horizontally) |
| *fl L or ‖* | Align type (vertically) |
| *tr #* | Transpose space (transfer) |
| *tr* | Transpose enclosed in ring (matter) |
| *tr ‖* | Transpose (order letters of or words) |
| *tr* | Rearrange words of order numbers in |
| *run over* | Run over to next line. (A two-letter di- over vision should be avoided) |
| *run back* | Run back to preceding line. (This div-sion is incorrect) |
| *reset* | A syllable or short word stand-ing alone on a line is called a "widow"; it should be eliminat-ed |
| *up* | |
| *up* | |
| *up* | |

### Paragraphing

| | |
|---|---|
| ¶ | Begin a paragraph |
| *no ¶* | No paragraph |
| *run in* | Run in or run on |
| ☐ ¶ | Indent the number of em quads shown |
| *flush ¶* | No paragraph indention |
| *hang in* | Hanging indention. This style should have all lines after the first marked for the desired indention |

### Punctuation

| | |
|---|---|
| ⊙ | Period or "full point." |
| | Periods and commas ALWAYS go inside quotes |
| ∧ or ⁄ | Comma   ⊙ or :⁄ Colon |
| | ;⁄ Semicolon |
| ∨ or ∨ | Apostrophe or 'single quote'   "*pos*" |
| ∨⁄∨ or ⁊⁊ | Quotation marks "quotes" |
| ?⁄ | Question mark or "query" |
| !⁄ | Exclamation point or "bang!" |
| -⁄ or =⁄ | Hyphen   *en* or ⁄ *em* En dash |
| *em* or ⊢ | One-em dash   ⊢ Two-em dash |
| (⁄) | Parentheses (parens; curves; fingernails) |
| [⁄] | Brackets (crotchets)   Brace |

### Miscellaneous

| | |
|---|---|
| *e⁄* | Correct letter or word marked |
| *e/⊗ k/⊗ or X* | Replace broken or imperfect type |
| ◉ | Reverse (upside-down type or cut) |
| ⊥ or ⊤ | Push down space or lead that prints |
| SP | Spell out (20 *gr*) (Also used conversely) |
| ?G | Question of grammar |
| ?F | Question of fact |
| *2u aa* or ?Au | Query to author (*2u ?*) |
| *2u Ed* | Query to editor (*2u Ed*) |
| | A ring around a marginal correction indicates that it is not the typesetter's error. All queries should be ringed |
| *OK w⁄c* or *OK. a⁄c* | OK "with corrections" Correct and print; no or "as corrected"   revised proof wanted |
| ⌐ | Mark-off or break; start new line |
| *End* | End of copy: #   or 30   or *End* |

**Figure 10-8:** Common proofreading marks.

**Figure 10-9:** Foundry type must be carefully distributed after it is printed.

cylinder and re-ink the type form each time a proof is pulled.

After the proof is pulled, the form must be cleaned with a cloth pad moistened with type wash (figure 10-7). Type wash is a solvent and is used to remove the ink that remains on the form after it is proofed. Type wash is also flammable. Be sure to place all rags containing solvents in a special metal safety can.

Standard proofreading marks (figure 10-8) are used to indicate changes and corrections on the proof that need to be made in the form. The common proofreading marks are shown and explained in figure 10-8. Use the marked proof as a guide for correcting the type form.

Some corrections can be made while the type form is still in the galley. These include replacing a broken letter, turning over an inverted letter, and changing letters of equal width. Tweezers may be used to remove and

insert letters but be careful not to damage the type.

Corrections that affect the length of the line can only be done with the form in the composing stick. Adding or deleting a word or replacing a letter with one having a different width are corrections that fall into this category.

When the form is no longer needed each piece of type must be returned to its proper location in the job case. This process is called <u>distribution</u>.

The proper technique for holding the type form during distribution is pictured in figure 10-9. Two or three lines of type are held in the left hand, nicks up. The top slug is removed and a complete word is picked off the right end of the form with the right hand. Each character of the word is then carefully dropped, one character at a time, into its proper location. Leads and slugs must also be returned to their proper locations.

---

### SELF CHECK

1. Describe the procedures for dumping and tying up a type form.
2. Prepare an outline of the steps to follow when proofing a type form.
3. Proofread a page in your notebook. Use standard proofreading marks to indicate changes and corrections that need to be made on this page.
4. Describe the procedures for distributing a type form.

Type and linoleum blocks must be locked up in a special metal frame before they can be used to reproduce multiple images on a letterpress (figure 11-1). This special metal frame is called a chase. The procedure for locking up a form by the chaser method is described below. This is the most commonly used method of lockup.

Forms are locked up on an imposing stone (figure 11-2). The stone is a steel-topped table. Its base contains compartments for storing the tools and materials used in lockup.

Begin by cleaning the surface of the imposing stone. This is done so all type characters will rest squarely on the stone's surface while the form is locked up.

**Figure 11-2:** An imposing stone is a steel-topped table on which lockup is done. (Hamilton Industries)

**Figure 11-1:** The form is locked up in a chase prior to being printed on a letterpress.

Place the type form on the stone by carefully sliding it from the galley. The head or top of the form should be nearest you or to your left. The position of the head is determined by the layout of the job.

Next surround the type form with a chase. The position of the form within the chase will depend upon the size and shape of the paper on which the image is to be printed. Try to position the form so it is slightly above the center of the chase. This will make it easier to feed the press with paper when the form is printed.

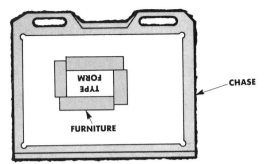

**Figure 11-3:** The chaser method of lockup. The type form is completely surrounded by wood or metal furniture.

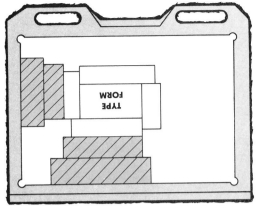

**Figure 11-4:** Fill in the space at the bottom and left of the type form with furniture.

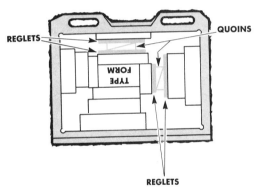

**Figure 11-5:** Quoins are positioned at the top and right sides of the type form. Reglets are used to protect the furniture.

After positioning the form in the chase, surround it with furniture as shown in figure 11-3. Furniture is wood or metal blocks used to fill the space between the type form and chase during lockup. Four pieces of furniture are used at first. They are placed clockwise around the form, overlapping at each corner. Each piece of furniture is slightly larger than the side against which it is placed. Each piece overlaps or chases the next piece of furniture around the form.

The space to the bottom and left of the type form is then filled with additional pieces of furniture. Use longer pieces of furniture as you approach the inner edges of the chase. Small spaces at the bottom and left of the chase are filled by sliding the type form and furniture down and toward the left (figure 11-4).

Next position quoins against the furniture at the top and right sides of the form. Quoins are wedge-shaped locks used to hold the form securely in the chase. Properly positioned quoins are pictured in figure 11-5. Place reglets (strips of wood 6 and 12 points thick) on either side of each pair of quoins. Reglets are used to protect the furniture when the quoins are tightened.

Once the quoins and reglets are in place, carefully remove the string from around the type form. Shift the furniture and quoins located at the top and

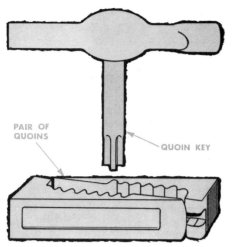

PAIR OF QUOINS

QUOIN KEY

**Figure 11-6:** A quoin key is used to tighten and loosen the quoins.

**Figure 11-7:** Plane the form to insure that all type characters are resting squarely on the stone.

right so that they rest firmly against the form. Fill in the remaining space at the top and right of the form with additional furniture.

Before tightening the quoins with a quoin key (figure 11-6), tighten each pair with your fingers. Then plane the form down with a planer (figure 11-7), to insure that all type characters are resting squarely on the stone. Place the flat surface of the planer on the form and gently tap it with the back of the quoin key. Be sure that all parts of the form are resting solidly on the stone.

After the form is planed, the quoins can be tightened with the quoin key. Tighten each quoin alternately, a little at a time. Repeat until the form is tight in the chase. Do not overtighten. Too much pressure on the quoins will crack the chase.

**Figure 11-8:** Testing for lift.

Test the lockup for tightness by carefully placing the end of the quoin key under one edge of the chase. Press down with your fingers on each line of type to determine any looseness. This is called testing for lift (figure 11-8). Loose lines of type must be rejustified before the form is printed.

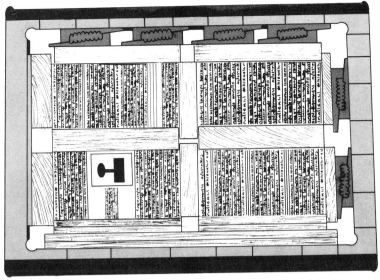

**Figure 11-9:** Four pages of type are locked up in this chase.

The term <u>imposition</u> refers to the process of positioning several type forms within a chase. The entire contents of the chase are then printed on a single sheet of paper. After printing, the paper may be folded and trimmed to form a booklet. If the type forms have been properly imposed, the pages of the booklet will appear in their correct order.

A chase containing four pages of type is pictured in figure 11-9. Note the furniture that has been added between each form. This is done to provide the necessary margins on each printed page. Note also that several quoins are used to hold the type forms securely in the chase.

### SELF CHECK

1. List in their proper sequence the basic steps involved in locking up a type form.
2. Prepare a simple diagram to illustrate the chaser method of lockup.
3. Describe what is meant by the term "imposition".
4. What is the difference between furniture and reglets?

Three types of presses are used to print letterpress forms and plates. They are:

- Platen press
- Cylinder press
- Rotary press

The operating principle of the <u>platen</u> <u>press</u> is shown in figure 12-1. The paper to be printed is placed on a flat surface called a platen. The type form

**Figure 12-2:** Hand-operated pilot press. (Brodhead-Garrett)

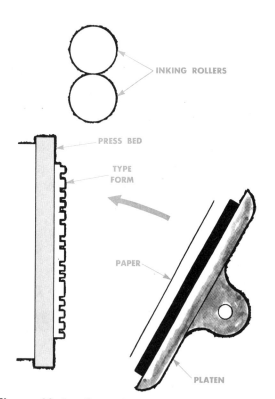

INKING ROLLERS

PRESS BED

TYPE FORM

PAPER

PLATEN

**Figure 12-1:** Operating principle of the platen press.

**Figure 12-3:** A hand-fed, power-operated platen press. (Brandtjen-Kluge, Inc.)

**Figure 12-4:** A power-operated platen press with automatic feed. (Heidelberg Eastern, Inc.)

or plate rests on another flat surface called the bed. Rollers ink the form each time the press is opened. When the press is closed, the paper is pressed against the type and the image transfers to the paper. Three kinds of platen presses are shown in figure 12-2 through 12-4.

Procedures for printing with a hand-fed, power-operated platen press are described here. Its parts have been labeled in figure 12-5. Operating procedures are grouped under four general categories:

- Preparation
- Makeready
- Operation
- Cleanup

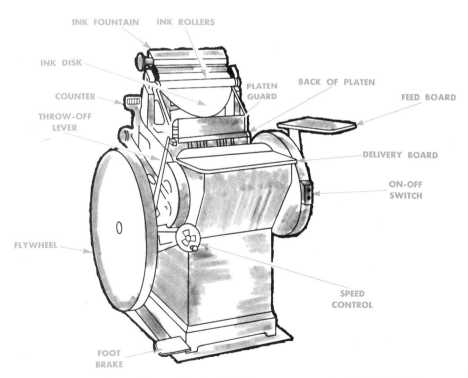

**Figure 12-5:** Parts of a hand-fed, power-operated platen press.

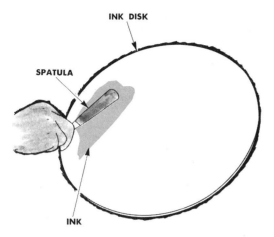

Figure 12-6: Ink the press by putting a small amount of ink on the ink disk.

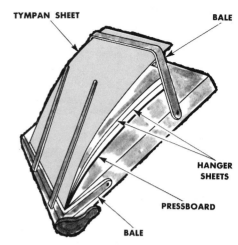

Figure 12-7: Dressing the press. The tympan sheet is held in position on the platen by the bales. Packing is placed under the tympan.

**Safety Note.** Before turning the press on, roll up your sleeves, remove your tie and make sure your shirttails are tucked in. Rings and watches should be removed. These items can all be caught by the press and cause you to be pulled into the machine.

The procedures that must be followed to prepare the press for printing are outlined below. The first step is to ink the press. Place a small quantity of ink on the lower left side of the ink disk, as shown in figure 12-6. Distribute the ink over the disk by turning the power on and allowing the press to run at slow speed. After the ink is distributed, turn off the press. The ink fountain is not used for short runs.

Dressing the press involves covering the platen with packing and a tympan or drawsheet. Packing consists of a piece of pressboard (smooth-finished hardboard) and several sheets of book paper. Check with your instructor to

determine the proper amount of packing to use. Packing should be cut slightly smaller than the size of the platen.

The tympan sheet holds the packing on the platen. It consists of a single piece of oiled manila paper. The width of the tympan should equal the width of the platen. It must be cut long enough to extend under the two bales as shown in figure 12-7.

Install the chase by turning the flywheel by hand until the rollers are in their lowest position. Carefully place the chase in the bed of the press. The clamp at the top of the bed must be pushed down over the edge of the chase. Quoins should be positioned to the top and right sides of the press, as shown in figure 12-8.

Check the position of the grippers. If they are in front of the type form when

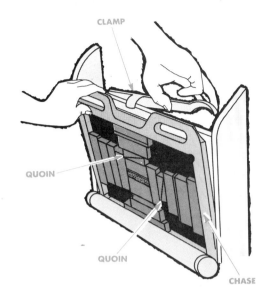

**Figure 12-8:** The chase is clamped in the bed of the press. Quoins are positioned to the top and right.

the impression is made, they will crush the type. Locate the grippers at the outer edges of the platen. Tighten the gripper nuts before proceeding.

Put the throw-off lever in the "off" position, turn the press on, and let it run slowly. When the type form has been inked, pull the throw-off lever to the "on" position and make one impression on the tympan sheet. Throw off the impression and turn off the press.

The image on the tympan will serve as a guide for positioning the paper. Draw center lines through the printed image as shown in figure 12-9. Next draw perpendicular lines on a piece of the paper on which the printing is to be done. The location of the point at which the lines cross should correspond

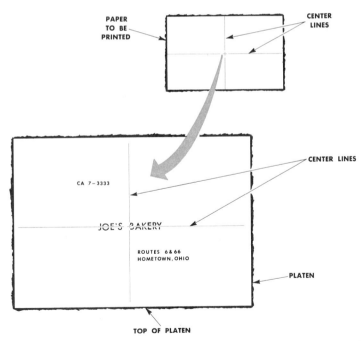

**Figure 12-9:** Center lines drawn through the image on the tympan will serve as a guide in positioning the paper.

to the center point of the image printed on the tympan. Place the paper on top of the tympan. Align the two sets of center lines and outline the paper on the tympan.

Gauge pins are devices that hold the paper in place on the platen. They are positioned to the bottom and left of the image on the tympan. Two pins are usually placed at the bottom and one at the left of the image. Insert the point of each gauge pin into the tympan about ⅛ inch outside of the paper border. Slide the point under the tympan and bring it back through the top surface. Do not penetrate the book paper. Align the edge of each gauge pin with the guidelines on the tympan. Properly positioned gauge pins are pictured in figure 12-10.

Be sure that the gauge pins will clear the type form. If they are in front of the form when the press is closed they will crush the type.

Place a sheet of paper against the gauge pins. Turn the press on and let it turn slowly. The throw-off lever should be in the "off" position. Once the type form has been inked, pull the throw-off lever to the "on" position and make an impression. Throw off the impression and turn off the press.

Check the position of the image on the paper. Use a ruler to insure accuracy. Move the gauge pins and repeat the above process until you get it right. Then set the gauge pins by tapping them lightly with a quoin key (figure 12-11).

The tympan image must be removed to prevent the ink on the tympan from transferring to the back of the printed sheets. Use a cloth moistened with solvent for this purpose. Apply talcum powder or chalk dust to the tympan to completely dry the just cleaned area.

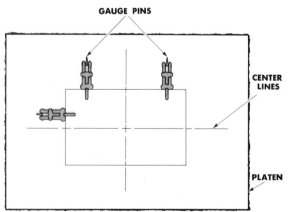

**Figure 12-10:** Gauge pins are used to hold the paper in place on the platen. They are positioned at the bottom and left sides of the tympan image.

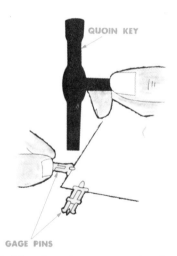

**Figure 12-11:** Set the gauge pins by tapping them with a quoin key.

Equalizing the impression on the paper is called <u>makeready</u>. To check the impression, place a sheet of paper against the gauge pins. Turn the press on and let it run slowly. Once the type form has been inked, pull the throw-off lever to the "on" position. After printing on the paper turn off the press. The impression on the paper should be clear and uniform.

If the image is not sharp and clear, it may be due to an incorrect ink supply. Rub your finger over the printed image. If there is too much ink, the image will smudge easily. Remove some ink from the ink disk. If the image does not smudge at all, ink needs to be added to the disk.

If the back of the printed sheet is embossed by the type form, then too much packing has been used. Remove one or more packing sheets.

The overall impression can be increased by adding one or more sheets to the packing. Be careful not to overpack the platen.

All parts of the form must print with a firm, even impression. Uniformity of impression may be obtained by pasting small pieces of tissue paper behind the tympan sheet (overlay) or by pasting small pieces of tissue paper behind the type form (underlay).

The grippers are used to hold the paper against the platen during printing. Position the grippers so that they will contact the paper and not the type form. A rubber band stretched across the two grippers can also be used to keep the paper in place on the platen.

The pile of paper to be printed is fanned out to separate the sheets and make them easy to pick up. The paper is then placed on the feed board. <u>Operating procedures</u> for a hand-fed, power-operated platen press are as follows:

1. Remove all tools and unnecessary materials from the press.
2. Set the impression counter at zero.
3. With the throw-off lever in the "off" position, turn on the power and let the press run at a slow speed.
4. Take a single sheet from the pile on the feed board with your right hand. Place the sheet in position on the platen by feeding it to the bottom gauge pins first, then sliding it against the side pin (figure 12-12).
5. With your left hand, pull the throw-off lever to the "on" position. After

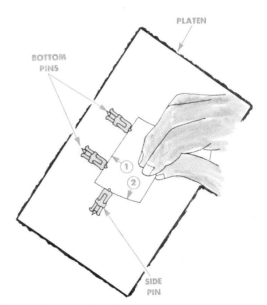

**Figure 12-12:** Feeding a platen press. Feed to the bottom gauge pins first. Then slide the paper to the left.

the impression is made, remove the printed sheet with your left hand and place it on the delivery table. At the same time position a fresh sheet of paper on the platen with your right hand. Another sheet of paper will be printed each time the platen closes. Caution! If a sheet is improperly positioned on the platen, the throw-off lever must be pushed to the "off" position. This is done to prevent printing on the tympan sheet. As the press opens, straighten the sheet, pull the throw-off lever to the "on" position, and resume printing.

**Safety Note.** Do not reach into a moving press to remove sheets, to apply ink, or make adjustments. Do not leave the press while it is running. Only one person should operate the press at a time. Avoid running the press at higher speeds than you can comfortably handle. When operating the press, stand erect, take your time, and concentrate on feeding and delivering the paper.

When you have finished, all ink must be removed from the ink disk and rollers before its dries. Press <u>cleanup procedures</u> follow:

1. Remove the chase from the press. Place it on the stone and wash the form with a suitable solvent.
2. Remove gauge pins, tympan, and packing from the platen. Be sure to close the bales before proceeding.
3. Saturate a cloth with solvent and use it to loosen the ink on the ink disk. Wipe the loosened ink from the disk with a sheet of newspaper.
4. Cover the ink disk with a fresh sheet of newspaper. Raise the ink rollers onto the disk by turning the flywheel by hand. Now use a clean cloth saturated with solvent to loosen and remove the ink on the rollers.

**Figure 12-14:** Flat-bed cylinder press used for reproduction proofing. (Vandersons Corp.)

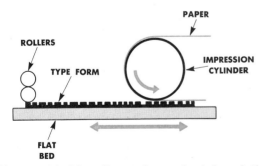

**Figure 12-13:** Operating principle of the cylinder press.

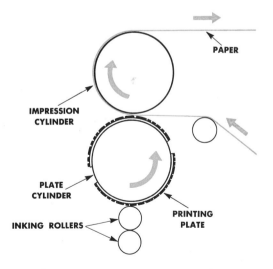

Repeat as required to remove all traces of ink from the press.

Do not leave the press with the rollers resting on the ink disk. Otherwise flat spots may develop on the ink rollers.

**Safety Note.** Place cloths containing solvents and inks in a special metal safety can.

The operating principle of the cylinder press is shown in figure 12-13. The type form is placed on a moving flat-bed. A rotating cylinder provides the necessary pressure. The paper is held in position around the cylinder by grippers during the printing operation. One type of cylinder press is pictured in figure 12-14.

The operating principle of the rotary press is shown in figure 12-15. Note that the printing plate is curved. Electrotypes, stereotypes, and rubber

plates may be used. The plate is held on one cylinder (the plate cylinder), while a second cylinder (the impression cylinder) provides the necessary pressure. The plate is inked as the plate cylinder rotates. A rotary press used to print newspapers is shown in figure 12-16.

Thermography is a technique that can be used to raise the image on a product printed by letterpress. The raised images found on business cards, announcements, and stationary are generally produced using this technique.

Thermography is easy to do. After printing, a special thermography powder is dusted on the still wet ink. Excess powder is removed and the printed item placed under a heating element. It remains under the element until the powder melts and fuses to the

**Figure 12-15:** Operating principle of the rotary press.

**Figure 12-16:** A rotary letterpress. (Rand McNally & Co.)

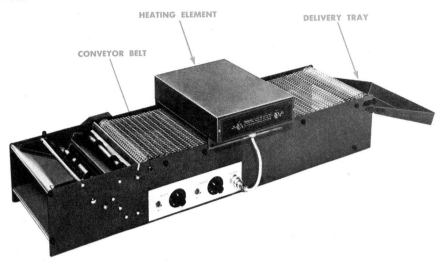

CONVEYOR BELT  HEATING ELEMENT  DELIVERY TRAY

**Figure 12-17:** A thermography machine is used to raise the image on a printed product.

image. The fused powder creates the raised image on the printed product. Powders used in thermography come in transparent, opaque, and metallic colors. The transparent powders allow the color of the base ink to show through. A machine used to heat the powder is pictured in figure 12-17.

**SELF CHECK**

1. Use simple diagrams to illustrate the operating principle of the platen press, the cylinder press, and the rotary press.
2. Outline the operating procedures for a hand-fed, power-operated platen press.
3. Explain what is meant by the term "makeready" and describe how to reduce impression, increase impression, and obtain a uniform impression.
4. Describe the procedures for raising a freshly printed image by the process of thermography.

Rubber stamps are easy to make. Type is set, a mold is made from the type, and the mold is used to create a relief image on the surface of a piece of rubber.

A press used to make rubber stamps is pictured in figure 13-1. Its major parts are two heated platens. The distance between the two platens is controlled by the handwheel at the right.

The steps in producing a rubber stamp are:

- Preparing the type form
- Making the matrix
- Forming the rubber
- Mounting the stamp

Hand-set foundry type or machine-set type may be used to <u>prepare the type form</u>. However, special type made for rubber stamp-making is preferred. It is made to withstand the heat and pressure needed to produce a rubber stamp. Making the matrix begins by locking the type form in the rubber stamp chase (figure 13-2). Follow the lockup procedures described in Unit 11. Use metal furniture in place of wood furniture, if available.

**Figure 13-1:** A rubber stamp press, chase, and vulcanizing tray is needed to make a rubber stamp. (Brodhead-Garrett Co.)

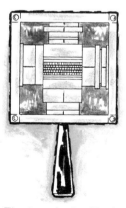

**Figure 13-2:** The type locked in the chase will be used to make a rubber stamp matrix.

Place the chase in the rubber stamp press and allow it to preheat for 2 minutes. The temperature of the platens should be 300° F. After 2 minutes remove the preheated form from the press and cover it with a piece of matrix board. The board should be approximately 1/4 inch larger than the type form on all sides. Its red or Bakelite side is placed against the type. After positioning the matrix board, cover its backside with a sheet of paper (figure 13-3). This will prevent the board from sticking to the upper platen of the press.

Insert the chase, matrix board, and paper cover into the press. Turn the handwheel clockwise until pressure is felt. Allow the matrix to heat for one minute and become soft. After one minute raise the bottom platen to the limit stops on the chase.

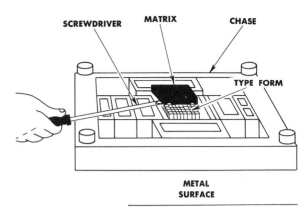

**Figure 13-4:** Remove the completed rubber stamp matrix from the type form.

After ten minutes remove the chase and matrix from the press. Carefully place it on a metal surface to cool. When cool, pry the matrix from the type form with a screwdriver (figure 13-4).

Forming the rubber is the next step. Cut a piece of stamp rubber to the size of the matrix. Peel off the protective cloth and dust the uncovered rubber surface with soapstone. This will keep the rubber from sticking to the matrix. Also dust the matrix with soapstone. Be sure to remove excess powder from the matrix before proceeding.

Place the matrix, image side up, on the vulcanizing tray. Cover the matrix with the powdered side of the stamp rubber. Place a sheet of paper over the back of the rubber to keep it from sticking to the platen (figure 13-5).

Insert the tray, matrix, rubber, and paper cover into the press. Turn the handwheel clockwise until the lower platen cannot be raised higher. Allow

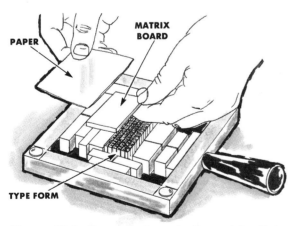

**Figure 13-3:** Preparing to make the matrix. Note that the matrix bcard is placed with its Bakelite side down on top of the type form. A piece of paper covers the matrix board.

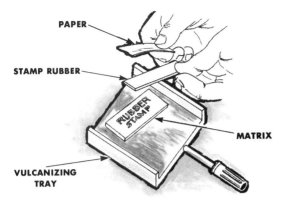

Figure 13-5: Preparing to form the rubber. Cover the matrix with stamp rubber and the rubber with paper.

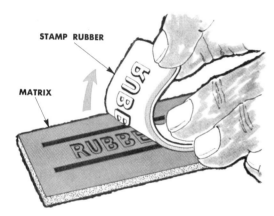

**Figure 13-6:** Stripping the rubber stamp from the matrix.

**Figure 13-7:** This rubber stamp has been properly made. All letters are clear with sharp edges.

Next, the rubber must be cut to size and <u>mounted</u> on a wooden handle. Use a backsaw to cut the handle to size.

Rubber cement is used to attach the stamp rubber to the spongelike pad of the handle. Coat the back of the rubber and the pad with rubber cement. Allow the cement on each surface to dry before pressing the surfaces together. A completed rubber stamp is pictured in figure 13-7.

| | **SELF CHECK** |
|---|---|

1. Prepare a simple diagram to illustrate the chaser method of locking up a type form for rubber stampmaking.
2. List in their proper sequence the basic steps in making a rubber stamp matrix.
3. List in their proper sequence the procedures that are followed when forming the rubber for a rubber stamp.
4. Describe how to mount a stamp on a wooden handle.

the stamp rubber to vulcanize for approximately six minutes.

Lower the bottom platen and carefully remove the vulcanizing tray and place it on a metal surface to cool. Once the rubber is cool, it can be stripped from the matrix, (figure 13-6).

# 3 PRINTING FROM A LOWERED SURFACE

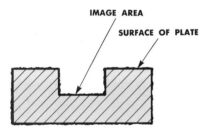

**Figure III-1:** In gravure printing the image area is cut below the surface of the plate.

Printing from a lowered surface is called <u>gravure printing</u>. The gravure process was invented over one hundred years ago. Today the gravure process is used to print Sunday newspaper supplements, magazines, mail order catalogs, stamps, and even paper money. Much of our printed fabric is also produced by gravure techniques. Intaglio (pronounced In-tal-yo) is another name for gravure printing.

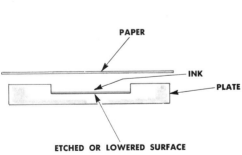

**Figure III-2:** Ink is transferred from the lowered surface of the plate to the paper. The top surface of the plate does not print because the ink has been removed.

In gravure printing, ink is transferred to paper from a lowered surface. The image area of a gravure plate is cut below or into the surface of the plate (figure III-1). The entire surface of the plate is inked and then wiped clean. This leaves ink in the lowered areas of the plate. Paper is then pressed against the plate and ink transfers to it (figure III-2). Paper is flexible. It can bend and stretch to get into the lowered areas of a gravure plate (figure III-3).

Like the raised image on a relief plate, the lowered image on a gravure

**Figure III-4:** The lowered surface of a gravure plate must be prepared in reverse. The symbols or characters on this plate are "wrong reading" or a mirror image of what is to be printed.

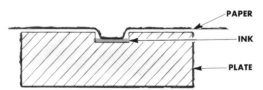

**Figure III-3:** Paper is flexible. It can bend and stretch to get into the lowered areas of a gravure plate.

plate must also be prepared in reverse. Look at figure III-4. Note the shape of the lowered surface that printed the letter P. It is "wrong reading" or backwards. The lowered surface was purposely prepared this way so that it would print a "right reading" image on the paper.

The image carriers or plates used in gravure printing are called <u>gravure plates</u>. Gravure plates can be made in two ways:

- Engraving
- Etching

<u>Engraved plates</u> are made by cutting designs into the surface of metal or plastic with hand tools.

The simplest type of engraving is the drypoint. A drypoint engraving is prepared by scratching a design into the surface of a clear plastic sheet. A pointed tool called a <u>scriber</u> is used for this purpose.

The first step in drypoint plate preparation is to select a design. Suitable designs are composed of lines only (figure 14-1). Solid areas of color cannot be reproduced by the drypoint technique.

The design must be transferred to the plate in reverse. This is necessary

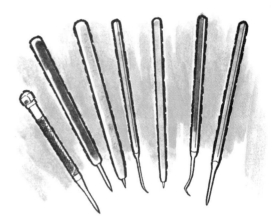

**Figure 14-2:** Several types of scribers.

to get a right-reading image when the plate is printed. Carbon paper placed carbon side up against the backside of the design can be used to reverse the image.

Tape the reversed design to a piece of transparent plastic. The plastic should be about 1 inch larger than the design, on all sides. The thickness of the plastic sheet can range between .015″ and .040″ thick.

A scriber (figure 14-2) is used to engrave the design. Deeply engraved lines will reproduce darker than shallow scratches. Shadow areas can be achieved by cross-hatching the engraved lines as shown in figure 14-3.

A drypoint plate in the process of being engraved is pictured in figure 14-4. Note the piece of black paper. It is placed between the design and plate to check for accuracy as the engraving progresses.

**Figure 14-1:** Designs made with fine lines are appropriate for drypoint engraving.

**Figure 14-3:** Cross-hatched areas will appear darker when the plate is printed.

**Figure 14-5:** This metal etching is ready to be printed.

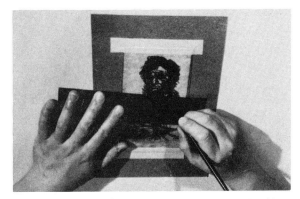

**Figure 14-4:** Lines are scratched into the dry-point plate with a scriber. Place a piece of black paper between the plate and design to check for accuracy.

After all lines have been engraved the plate is ready to be printed. Printing procedures are described in the next unit.

Acid can also be used to cut a design into the surface of a piece of metal. This is called etching. The simplest type of gravure plate is the metal etching.

A metal etching (figure 14-5) is prepared by first coating the surface of a metal sheet with a resist. A resist is a material that acid cannot penetrate. The design is then scratched through the resist with a scriber. The scriber cuts through the resist only. The bare metal that is exposed in this manner represents the design.

The metal sheet is then placed into an acid bath. Areas of the sheet that are protected by the resist are not affected by the acid. However, the unprotected areas are dissolved away, forming a gravure image on the etched plate.

Almost any metal can be used, but aluminum is recommended. Aluminum is easy to etch. Make certain that the metal is clean and free of fingerprints.

Apply a resist to both sides of the aluminum. This is done to keep the back of the metal from being etched away when it is placed in the acid bath. Allow the resist to dry before proceeding.

Designs suitable for engraving are also suitable for etching. They must be transferred to the plate in reverse. Carbon paper is used for this purpose.

Using a scriber scratch the design through the resist. Make sure the scratches are deep enough to expose the metal. Do not cut into the aluminum.

Place the aluminum plate in an aluminum etching solution with tongs.

**Safety Note:** Wear safety glasses and rubber gloves when working with etching solutions. Always add acid to water when mixing the etching solution. Do not add water to acid. A violent reaction may occur.

**Figure 14-6:** Etching the metal plate.

**Figure 14-7:** A gravure cylinder. (Gravure Technical Association, Inc.)

A plate in the process of being etched is shown in figure 14-6. The longer the plate remains in the etching bath, the deeper the depressions in the surface of the plate. Deep depressions reproduce darker than shallow ones.

When the desired depth has been achieved, remove the plate from the etching bath and wash it under running water to remove all traces of etching solution. Remove the resist with a suitable solvent, and the plate is ready to be printed.

Gravure cylinders (figure 14-7) are also prepared by etching away the unprotected areas of a piece of metal. This time, however, the metal is cylindrical in shape. Because the image may be located completely around the cylinder, continuous patterns can be printed on products such as wall coverings and textiles. Paper money and postage stamps are also printed from gravure cylinders as are many magazines and catalogs. Printing from gravure cylinders is discussed in the next unit.

**SELF CHECK**

1. List in their proper sequence the steps involved in preparing a drypoint plate.
2. Describe the procedures for preparing a metal etching.
3. Identify the safety precautions to be taken when etching a metal plate.
4. Explain the differences between engravings and etchings.

Two types of presses are used to print gravure plates:

- Engraving and etching press
- Rotogravure press

An engraving and etching press with its major parts identified is pictured in figure 15-1. This type of press is used to print drypoint engravings and metal etchings.

The plate is inked and placed on the bed of the press. It is then covered with a dampened sheet of paper and a felt blanket. Pressure, applied by the impression roller, causes the ink to transfer to the paper.

Begin by preparing the paper. Cut several pieces of soft, uncoated paper, like mimeograph stock, to size. The dimensions of the paper should be at least two inches wider and two inches longer than the dimensions of the plate. Place the paper, one sheet at a time, into a tray of water.

Next prepare the ink. Place a small amount of letterpress ink on a glass

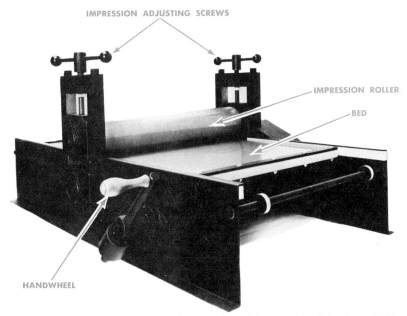

**Figure  15-1:** The parts of an engraving and etching press. (Rembrandt Graphic Arts)

**Figure 15-2:** Inking a drypoint plate. Force the ink into the lines with a dauber.

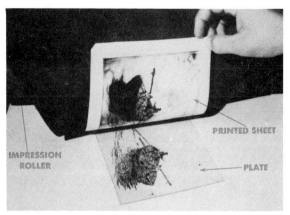

PRINTED SHEET

IMPRESSION ROLLER

PLATE

**Figure 15-3:** Strip the printed sheet from the plate after it passes under the impression roller.

plate. Add a drop or two of linseed oil. Use an ink knife to thoroughly mix the ink and the linseed oil.

Inking the plate is the next step. Use a dauber, a piece of folded cloth, or your fingertips to ink the plate. Force the ink into the lowered image areas. Completely fill these areas with ink. (figure 15-2).

Ink on the surface of the plate must now be removed. Use a clean wiping cloth, folded to form a pad, to remove ink from the plate's surface. The heel of your hand may also be used to clean the non-printing areas of the plate. Be careful not to remove ink from the lowered, image areas.

You are now ready to print the plate. Place the inked plate, face up, on the bed of the press. Remove a sheet of paper from the water tray and place it on a piece of blotter paper. Blot with a second piece of blotter paper and cover the printing plate with the dampened

sheet of paper. Finally, place a felt blanket over the paper.

Now turn the hand wheel of the press until the lead edge of the plate is just under the impression roller. Hand tighten the impression adjusting screws to increase the pressure on the paper and plate. Turn the hand wheel until the plate emerges on the other side of the impression roller. Strip the printed sheet from the plate and place it on a rack to dry (figure 15-3). Repeat the steps above to make more prints.

The plate must be cleaned if it is to be printed again. Use solvent to remove all ink from the plate.

The operating principle of the rotogravure press is shown in figure 15-4. A gravure cylinder is used as the plate. Image areas are filled with a thin ink as the gravure cylinder revolves in an ink bath. A fine steel squeegee, called a doctor blade, is used to remove excess ink from the surface or non-image areas of the cylinder. A

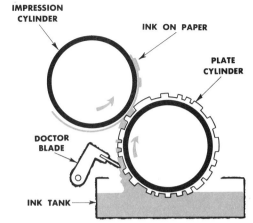

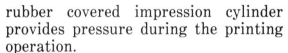

**Figure 15-4:** Operating principle of the rotogravure press.

**Figure 15-5:** A web-fed, multi-color rotogravure press used for magazine printing. (Southern Gravure Service, Inc.)

rubber covered impression cylinder provides pressure during the printing operation.

The paper to be printed can be supplied to the press in sheets or in rolls. A roll or web-fed, multi-color rotogravure press is shown in figure 15-5.

## SELF CHECK

1. Describe how to prepare the paper and ink used in printing engravings and etchings.
2. List the steps to be followed when printing with an engraving and etching press.
3. Prepare a simple diagram to illustrate how a rotogravure press operates. Label each of the major parts of this press.
4. What is a doctor blade?

# PRINTING FROM A FLAT SURFACE

You have already learned how printing can be done from a raised surface and from a lowered surface. Do you think it's possible to print from a flat surface? The answer is yes.

Printing from a flat surface is called lithographic printing or lithography. Alois Senefelder of Germany discovered this printing technique in 1796. Today more things are printed by lithography than by any other printing method.

Lithographic printing is based on the principle that grease and water do not mix (figure IV-1). The process works this way. A greasy image is placed on a flat plate. The image may be drawn directly on the plate with a grease pencil. It can also be placed on the plate by photographic means.

Next, water is applied to the plate. This water will cover the non-image area of the plate. The water will not cover the greasy image because water and grease do not mix!

The entire plate is then coated with ink. Ink is a greasy substance and adheres to the greasy image. The ink

**Figure IV-1:** Grease and water do not mix. If you have ever tried to wash greasy hands with just water you know that grease and water don't mix.

does not adhere to the wet portions of the plate because grease and water do not mix!

Paper is then pressed against the surface of the plate and the inked image is transferred to the paper. The process of printing from a flat surface is shown in figure IV-2.

Lithography is printing from a plane or flat surface, one which is neither

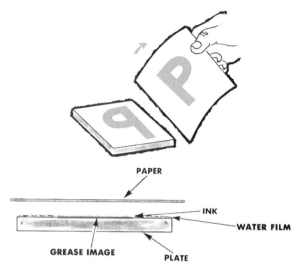

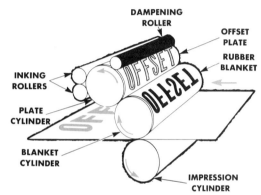

**Figure IV-2:** Lithographic printing is done from a flat surface.

**Figure IV-4:** The paper receives the image from the blanket. The paper does not contact the printing plate in offset lithography.

**Figure IV-3:** Offset printing. The image is first transferred from the plate to a rubber blanket.

**Figure IV-5:** The major parts of an offset lithographic press.

raised nor depressed. The printing image is formed chemically by making some areas of the plate <u>grease receptive</u>, while other areas are <u>water receptive.</u> Unlike plates for letterpress and gravure printing (which have their printing surfaces shaped to form the desired image), the printing image on a lithographic plate simply rests upon the plate's surface.

The image can rapidly wear away when paper rubs against it during the printing process. This is especially true when the plates are used on high-speed printing presses. To minimize wear in such a situation, the image on the plate is first <u>offset</u> (transferred) to a rubber blanket (figure IV-3). Figure IV-4 shows how the paper receives the image from the blanket. The paper does not make contact with the printing plate. The entire offset lithographic process is shown in figure IV-5.

Several techniques are used to make the letters and numbers to be printed by lithography.

Letters and numbers can be generated without the use of type made from hot, molten metal. This is called cold-type composition. Cold-type composition may be done in three ways:

- Hand-assembling preprinted letters
- Using a typewriter
- Photographically

A variety of preprinted alphabets are available for composing type by hand. These materials are inexpensive, but if properly used produce professional looking copy.

```
ABCDEFGHIJKLMNOPQRSTUVWXYZAEIOU :;
ABCDEFGHIJKLMNOPQRSTUVWXYZAEIOU :;
ABCDEFGHIJKLMNOPQRSTUVWXYZAEIOU :;
ABCDEFGHIJKLMNOPQRSTUVWXYZAEIOU :;
ABCDEFGHIJKLMNOPQRSTUVWXYZAEIOU :;
ABCDEFGHIJKLMNOPQRSTUVWXYZAEIOU :;
ABCDEFGHIJKLMNOPQRSTUVWXYZAEIOU :;
11234567890123456789012345678900 0000
11234567890123456789012345678900 0000
abcdefghijklmnopqrstuvwxyzabcdefghijklm n
abcdefghijklmnopqrstuvwxyzabcdefghijklm n
abcdefghijklmnopqrstuvwxyzabcdefghijklm n
abcdefghijklmnopqrstuvwxyzabcdefghijklm n
abcdefghijklmnopqrstuvwxyzabcdefghijklm n
abcdefghijklmnopqrstuvwxyzabcdefghijklm n
abcdefghijklmnopqrstuvwxyzabcdefghijklm n
opqrstuvwxyz opqrstuvwxyz opqrstuvwxyz&$
```

**Figure 16-1:** Dry-transfer type. The preprinted characters are attached to a carrier sheet.

Dry-transfer type (figure 16-1) consists of preprinted characters attached to the back of a transparent plastic or paper sheet. Each sheet usually contains a single size and style of type. The desired letter is positioned over a piece of white paper, and transferred by rubbing the top of the sheet with a smooth, blunt tool such as the end of a ball point pen (figure 16-2).

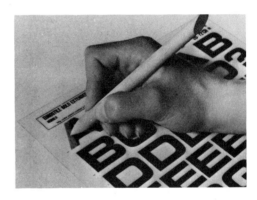

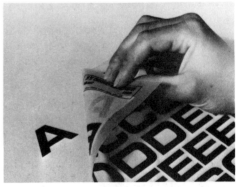

**Figure 16-2:** Dry-transfer composition. The character is placed over the mechanical, rubbed, and the carrier sheet is pulled away. (Zipatone Inc.)

**Figure 16-3:** Pressure-sensitive type composition. The letter is cut out of the carrier sheet and adhered to the mechanical. (FORMATT Cut-out Acetate Art Aids)

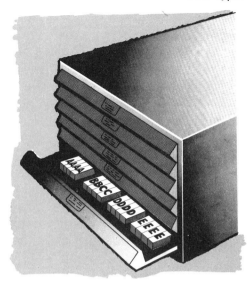

**Figure 16-4:** Hand-set paper type is supplied as preprinted letters on paper pads.

Pressure sensitive types (figure 16-3) consist of letters printed on clear plastic sheets. Each sheet contains a single size and style of type. The back of the sheet is coated with an adhesive and protected by a paper backing sheet. Letters are cut out of the sheet with a sharp knife, positioned on paper, and rubbed to make them stick.

Hand-set paper type (figure 16-4) is supplied as preprinted letters on paper pads. Each pad contains a number of single letters. Pads are available in a wide variety of type styles and sizes. Letters are removed from the pads and assembled in a special composing stick (figure 16-5). Start at the closed end of the stick and push each new letter against the one before it. The blue side should face up. Letters on the other side of the sheets are printed in black ink. Blanks are used to space between words.

**Figure 16-5:** Hand-set paper type is set by removing characters from their pads and assembling them in a special composing stick.

Completed lines of type are removed from the stick with tape. Cut a piece of tape a little longer than the line and lay it over the letters. Remove the type from the stick and turn it over so the black printed letters face up.

<u>Typewriters</u> are cold-type typesetting machines. Reproducible images are made by an operator depressing keys on the typewriter keyboard. As each key is depressed a raised character strikes an inking ribbon, causing the ribbon to contact a sheet of paper. The image is formed when ink is transferred from the ribbon to the paper.

Standard typewriters may be used to compose type matter. They are limited, however, because all characters on a standard typewriter occupy the same amount of space. This limitation has been overcome by the proportional spacing typewriter (figure 16-6).

A second limitation is that the type face on a standard typewriter cannot be changed. With the development of

**Figure 16-7:** An IBM "Selectric Composer" features proportional spacing and interchangeable type faces. It will automatically justify type matter during a second typing. (IBM Office Products Division)

```
Standard typewriters can beXX
used to produce justifiedXXXXX
type matter. This isXXXXXXXX
accomplished by typing theXXX
copy twice. Decide on aXXXXX
maximum line length and begin
typing. Do not exceed theXXX
desired line length on anyXXX
line typed. Stop typing when
you near the end of a lineXXX
and there is not enough roomX
to add another full word.XXXX
Fill in the space remainingXX
on each line with a series of
X's. The X's representXXXXX
spaces to be added betweenXXX
words during the secondXXXXXX
typing.
```

```
Standard typewriters can be
used to produce justified
type matter. This is
accomplished by typing the
copy twice. Decide on a
maximum line length and begin
typing. Do not exceed the
desired line length on any
line typed. Stop typing when
you near the end of a line
and there is not enough room
to add another full word.
Fill in the space remaining
on each line with a series of
X's. The X's represent
spaces to be added between
words during the second
typing.
```

**Figure 16-8:** Justifying type matter with a standard typewriter. Two typings are required. The X's represent spaces to be added during the second typing.

**Figure 16-6:** A proportional spacing typewriter. (IBM Office Products Division)

interchangeable typeface typewriters (figure 16-7), this limitation has also been overcome.

If necessary, standard typewriters can be used to produce justified type matter. The process of justifying type matter with a standard typewriter is shown in figure 16-8.

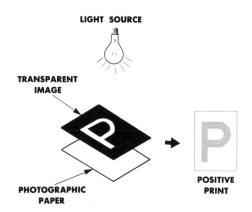

**Figure 16-9:** The basic principle of photocomposition. Light-sensitive paper is exposed to a source of light through a film negative of the character.

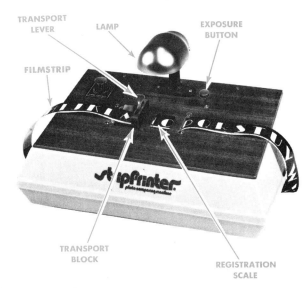

**Figure 16-10:** The StripPrinter is used for display composition. (StripPrinter Inc.)

**Figure 16-11:** Registration marks on the StripPrinter filmstrip serve as an aid in letter spacing.

Typesetting by means of photography is called <u>photocomposition</u> (figure 16-9). Characters are generated by exposing photographic paper through a series of negatives. Each negative contains a transparent image of a character.

Photocomposition is done on phototypesetting machines. Some phototypesetters produce display type—others generate text type. Still others produce both display type and text type.

Display phototypesetters produce display type. Display type measures 14 points and larger and is used for headlines or to attract attention. Two display phototypesetters are discussed here.

A <u>StripPrinter</u> (figure 16-10) has a filmstrip containing one size and style of type that serves as the negative. A roll of light-sensitive paper is positioned within the unit's housing, directly below the lamp. The lamp controls exposure.

Registration marks (figure 16-11) for letter spacing are provided on the filmstrip. Each character has a left and right registration mark. The distance between left and right registration marks is slightly larger than the width of the character.

Setting type with a StripPrinter is easy. Position the filmstrip so the first

character to be set is between the lamp and sensitized paper. Align the left registration mark of the character with the zero mark on the registration scale. Lock the transport block with the transport lever. Move the transport block to the left until the registration mark at the right of the character aligns with the zero mark on the registration scale. Locking and moving the transport block also advances the light-sensitive paper.

Exposure is made by pressing the exposure button. Repeat the positioning and exposure process until all of the desired characters have been set.

**Figure 16-12:** This machine can be used to process the light-sensitive paper that is exposed in the StripPrinter.

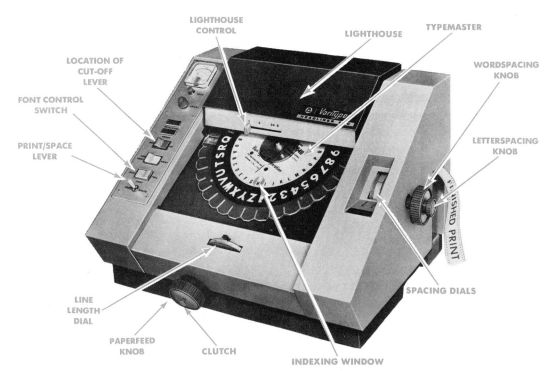

**Figure 16-13:** The Headliner automatically provides the correct amount of space between display characters. The depth of the slots along the edge of the Typemaster disk control letter spacing. (Addressograph-Multigraph Corp.)

Then remove the exposed paper from the StripPrinter and process it in a darkroom or in a processor (figure 16-12).

A <u>Headliner</u> (figure 16-13) also produces images by means of contact printing. Unlike the StripPrinter, however, it automatically adjusts the space between characters.

A plastic disc containing one size and style of type serves as the negative. Slots of varying depth are located along the outside of the disk. These slots control letter spacing.

Place the disk on the Headliner. Set the wordspacing dial, the lighthouse setting, and the full- or half-font control switch according to the directions on the disk.

Turn the disk until the correct character appears in the indexing window. Expose the light-sensitive paper, which is located below the lighthouse, by moving the print-space lever to the print position. The light-sensitive paper advances automatically when the print lever is moved. Repeat this procedure until all of the characters have been set.

After composition has been completed, cut off the exposed paper by lifting the cut-off lever. The paper is automatically fed into a self-contained processing tank. Here it is developed, fixed, and washed before emerging from the side of the Headliner.

Text phototypesetters (figure 16-14) are used to compose text type. Text type measures 12 points and smaller and is used for the body of a page or book.

**Figure 16-14:** A phototypesetter used for text composition. (Addressograph-Multigraph Corp.)

### SELF CHECK

1. Describe what is meant by the term dry-transfer type and explain how it is used.
2. Describe what is meant by pressure-sensitive type and explain how it is used.
3. List in outline form the procedures for composing type matter with hand-set paper type.
4. List in outline form the procedures to be followed when composing justified type matter on a standard typewriter.

The image area on a lithographic plate is grease receptive and water repellent. It attracts oil-base inks and repels water. The non-image area is water receptive and grease repellent. It attracts water and repels oil-base inks (figure 17-1).

The three most commonly used types of lithographic plates are:

- Direct-Image Plates
- Diffusion-Transfer Plates
- Presensitized Plates

Lithographic plates may be prepared in several ways. One way is to type or draw the image directly on a paper or plastic surface. Plates prepared in this manner are called direct-image plates.

The direct-image plate (figure 17-2) is usually made from paper or plastic. The surface of the plate is treated to accept the grease image. This treatment also increases the printing life of the plate and makes non-image areas more receptive to water.

Almost any greasy substance can be used to place an image on a plate. Grease pencils, crayons, and typewriters fitted with special ribbons are most often used for this purpose.

Typing is done with a typewriter. Keep the typewriter clean. Avoid transferring fingerprints to the plate's surface.

Place the plate in the typewriter. Position the plate and begin to type. Use a low-impression setting to avoid embossing the plate. A soft eraser may be used to remove errors.

Illustrations and hand lettering can be added to a direct-image plate with special pens and pencils. Nonreproducing pencils may be used to provide drawing guidelines.

Diffusion-transfer plates are made from a mechanical. A mechanical or pasteup (figure 17-3) is an exact duplicate of the job to be printed. It contains completed illustrations and type matter.

Pictures and type are assembled on a suitable base to produce the mechanical. The comprehensive layout serves as a guide or blueprint.

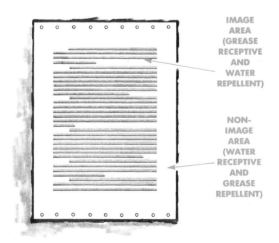

IMAGE AREA (GREASE RECEPTIVE AND WATER REPELLENT)

NON-IMAGE AREA (WATER RECEPTIVE AND GREASE REPELLENT)

**Figure 17-1:** The parts of a lithographic plate.

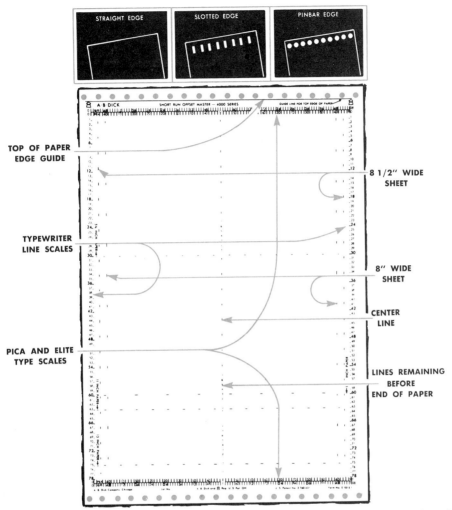

**Figure 17-2:** The guidelines on this direct-image plate serve as an aid to the typist. They do not reproduce when the plate is printed.

A clean, white piece of illustration board can be used as a base. White cardstock may also be used. Trim the base so that it is at least one inch longer and one inch wider than the size of the final product.

Use a light blue pencil to mark the locations of the elements. Light blue lines do not have to be erased. They will photograph as if they were white.

Apply a thin, even coat of rubber cement to the back of each element

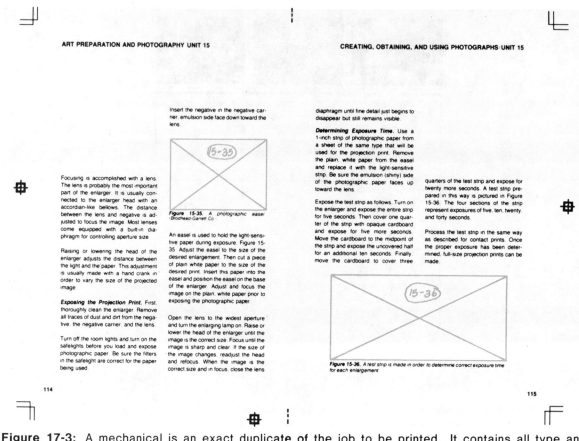

**Figure 17-3:** A mechanical is an exact duplicate of the job to be printed. It contains all type and illustrations.

with a small brush. Place the elements on the base and press lightly with your fingertips. Excess rubber cement can be removed after it is dry. Rub gently and make sure your hands are clean.

Wax may also be used to adhere the elements to the base. A wax-coating machine such as the one pictured in figure 17-4 is used to apply a thin layer of wax to the back of each element. The element is then attached to the base. If necessary, elements can be removed and repositioned.

**Figure 17-4:** A wax-coating machine. It is used to apply a thin layer of wax to the backs of the elements that are to be adhered to the mechanical. (Challenge Machinery Co.)

**Figure 17-5:** A machine for exposing and processing diffusion-transfer plates. (Scriptomatic, Inc.)

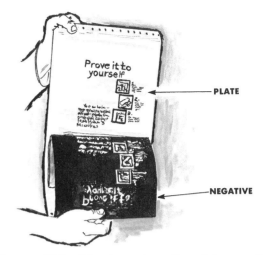

**Figure 17-6:** The image on the plate results when unexposed silver crystals are transferred from the negative and developed on the plate.

In the diffusion-transfer process a paper negative is produced directly from the mechanical by a contact printing technique. The negative is then placed in contact with a flexible metal plate and developed. As the paper negative develops, its unexposed areas transfer to the flexible plate. These areas form the image on the plate.

A platemaking machine that operates on the principle of diffusion-transfer is pictured in figure 17-5. It consists of two basic units: an exposure unit and a processing unit.

The paper negative is placed, emulsion side up, on the glass plate of the exposure unit. The mechanical is positioned, image side down, on top of the paper negative. The negative is now ready to be exposed. Closing the lid of the exposure unit automatically creates a vacuum, and exposes the negative. Exposure results from light passing through the paper negative, striking the white areas on the mechanical, and reflecting back onto the emulsion of the negative.

After exposure, the negative is processed by placing the metal plate, face up, at the entrance to the processing unit. The paper negative is positioned above the plate, emulsion side down, and fed into the processer. When the plate and negative emerge, the plate will contain image areas that duplicate those of the original copy (figure 17-6).

After about a minute, the negative is stripped from the plate. The plate is then desensitized and lacquered as shown in figure 17-7. The plate is now ready to be placed on the offset press. If the plate will not be printed immediately, coat its surface with gum arabic.

**Figure 17-7:** The diffusion-transfer plate must be desensitized and lacquered before printing. Use chemicals as recommended by the manufacturer of the plate.

**Figure 17-9:** A vertical process camera. Major parts are all arranged on a vertical axis. (NuArc Co., Inc.)

**Figure 17-8:** A horizontal process camera. Major parts are all arranged on a horizontal axis. (NuArc Co., Inc.)

Presensitized plates are coated with a light-sensitive emulsion. The image is placed on the plate's surface photographically, by contact printing through a film negative of a mechanical.

Process photography is the technique used to convert the mechanical into the film negative. The equipment, materials, and procedures utilized in process photography are described below:

The process camera is used to photograph the mechanical. The negative image that results may be made larger, smaller, or the same size as the image on the mechanical.

There are two types of process cameras, horizontal (figure 17-8) and vertical (figure 17-9). The major parts of a

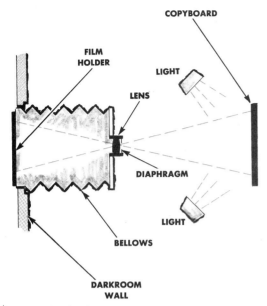

**Figure 17-10:** Parts of a process camera.

process camera are illustrated in figure 17-10.

Many kinds of film are available for process photography. All produce high-contrast negatives. High-contrast negatives consist of black areas and clear areas. Grays or tones are not recorded by high contrast film.

Orthochromatic film is used for general process work. Orthochromatic film is not sensitive to red light. It can be handled in the darkroom under safelight conditions.

Line negatives are prepared by photographing line copy. Line copy is any copy that contains no shades of grey. The images are formed by lines and areas of single tone. Examples of

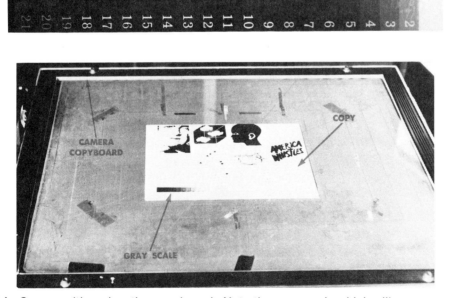

**Figure 17-11:** Copy positioned on the copyboard. Note the grey scale which will serve as a guide when the film is developed.

line copy include most type matter, pen and ink drawings, and photographs that have already been screened. Such prescreened photographs are called veloxes.

The procedures for exposing a line negative are as follows:

- Clean the Camera—All dust and dirt must be removed from the camera's copyboard, lens, and film holder before exposing the negative. Dust can cause pinholes in the emulsion of the negative.
- Position the Copy—Center the copy on the copyboard. Place a grey scale within the white area of the copy (figure 17-11). This grey scale will serve as a helpful guide when the film is developed. Close the cover glass and turn the copyboard—it must be parallel to the camera's lens and film holder.

- Focus the Camera—The camera must be set to obtain the desired reduction or enlargement. This is done by adjusting the distance between the lens and film holder and between the lens and copyboard. Focusing controls are provided for this purpose. When properly set the image on the film will be correctly sized and in sharp focus.

- Adjust the Lens Aperture—The size of the lens aperture or opening determines the intensity of the light that will enter the camera. Aperture size is controlled by a diaphragm. $f$/numbers (figure 17-12) are used to indicate the various openings that are formed by adjusting the diaphragm. Each lens has its own "best" aperture for photographic reproduction. It

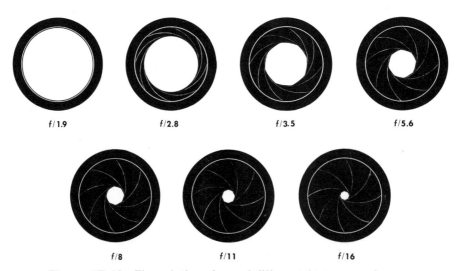

f/1.9     f/2.8     f/3.5     f/5.6

f/8     f/11     f/16

**Figure 17-12:** The relative sizes of different $f$/stop openings.

is the "best" aperture because it yields sharp, clear negatives while keeping exposure time to a minimum. Ask your teacher about the "best" aperture for your camera.

- Set the Timer—A timer is used to control the length of exposure. The timer automatically opens and closes the shutter. It usually controls the camera's lights as well. Length of exposure depends on several things. One is the strength of the lights. Another is the type of film being used. The amount of enlargement or reduction also affects exposure. Ask your teacher for the correct exposure time to produce your negative.

- Load the Film—Turn off all white lights in the darkroom and turn on the safelights. Remove a sheet of film from the film box and cut it to size. Film size should be slightly larger than the size of the image. Handle the film by its edges only. Place the film, emulsion side up, on the center of the film holder. Loading is completed by turning on the vacuum pump and closing the film holder.

- Expose the Film—Press the exposure button. The camera's lights will go on and the shutter will open. After the exposure is completed, the shutter closes and the lights go off. At this point you can open the film holder, switch off the vacuum pump, and remove the film for processing.

**Figure 17-13:** A continuous-tone photograph contains gradations in tone. Tones range from white, through the various shades of gray, to black.

**Figure 17-14:** An enlarged section of figure 17-13. Note how the image is formed by black dots. The sizes of these dots vary.

Halftone negatives are prepared by photographing continuous-tone copy. Examples of continuous-tone copy include most photographic prints and wash drawings. Note that the image of the photograph shown in figure 17-13 is made up of black areas, white areas, and areas that are grey.

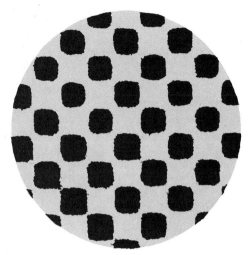

**Figure 17-15:** An enlarged section of a contact screen. The screen is made up of dots with fuzzy edges.

**Figure 17-16:** A 85-line screen was used to produce this photograph.

**Figure 17-17:** This photograph was prepared using a 150-line screen.

Compare figure 17-13 with figure 17-14. Figure 17-14 is an enlargement of a portion of figure 17-13. Note how the image is formed by various sizes of dots. The dots are printed in black ink only.

Halftone negatives are needed to make plates that will reproduce continuous-tone copy. These negatives are made by exposing process film to light, reflecting from continuous-tone copy, through a special contact screen. An enlarged view of a contact screen is shown in figure 17-15.

Contact screens are classified according to the number of dots they produce on each linear inch of film. A photograph reproduced with a 85-line screen is shown in figure 17-16. The same photograph, prepared with a 150-line screen, is shown in figure 17-17.

During exposure, the emulsion of the contact screen is placed in direct contact with the emulsion of the process film. Light reflecting from the continuous-tone copy must pass through the screen to create an image on the film. Different areas of the copy reflect different amounts of light. The intensity of the light passing through the con-

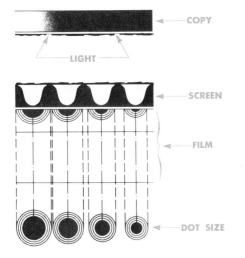

**Figure 17-18:** Forming the halftone dot. Light reflecting from the continuous-tone copy passes through the contact screen and strikes the film. The size of the dot formed on the film is determined by the intensity of the light reflecting from the copy.

tact screen will determine both the size and shape of the halftone dots (figure 17-18).

Line and halftone negatives are generally processed under red safelights. Three trays are used. The first tray is filled with developer, the second contains stop, and the third tray is filled with fixer. A large tray or tank in which to wash the processed negatives is also required. A typical set-up is shown in figure 17-19.

After processing, the negatives are attached to a special type of paper called goldenrod. Arranging and mounting negatives on goldenrod is termed stripping. Goldenrod with negatives attached is called a flat. The flat is used to hold the negatives in position while burning (exposing) the presensitized plate. Procedures for stripping follow:

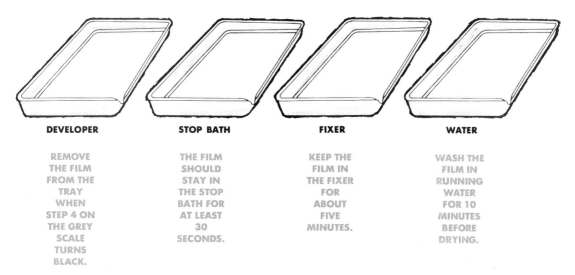

| DEVELOPER | STOP BATH | FIXER | WATER |
|---|---|---|---|
| REMOVE THE FILM FROM THE TRAY WHEN STEP 4 ON THE GREY SCALE TURNS BLACK. | THE FILM SHOULD STAY IN THE STOP BATH FOR AT LEAST 30 SECONDS. | KEEP THE FILM IN THE FIXER FOR ABOUT FIVE MINUTES. | WASH THE FILM IN RUNNING WATER FOR 10 MINUTES BEFORE DRYING. |

**Figure 17-19:** A typical tray setup for processing line and halftone negatives.

**Figure 17-20:** A light table is used for stripping a flat. (NuArc Co., Inc.)

**Figure 17-21:** The dimensions of the paper and the location of the image to be printed have been marked on this piece of goldenrod.

**Figure 17-22:** After positioning the negative, tape it by its corners to the goldenrod sheet.

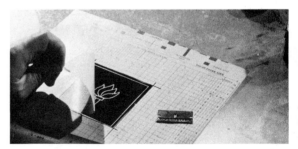

**Figure 17-23:** The size of the window should be 1/8″ to 1/4″ larger than the image on the negative.

Using a T-square, align the goldenrod on the glass surface of a light table (figure 17-20). Fasten its corners to the glass with tape.

Locate the line on the goldenrod that corresponds to the top edge of the paper to be printed. Using this line as a starting point, locate and mark the left, right, and bottom dimensions of the paper. Now mark the position of the image to be printed (figure 17-21).

Place the negative, emulsion side up, on the goldenrod. Place the image within the marked area. Tape its corners to the goldenrod (figure 17-22).

Detach the goldenrod from the glass top and turn it over. Using a sharp razor blade, cut a window (figure 17-23) into the goldenrod. Cut through the

**Figure 17-24:** Opaquing is done in order to cover pinholes and other unwanted transparent areas in the negative.

**Figure 17-25:** A flip-top platemaker. (NuArc Co., Inc.)

goldenrod only. Do not cut into the negative. The size of the window should be ⅛″ to ¼″ larger than the image on the negative. After cutting, remove the piece of goldenrod from within the window area.

Opaquing (figure 17-24) is done on a light table. Place the flat, with the emulsion side of the negative down, on the glass top. Use a fine brush and photographic opaquing solution to cover all pinholes and other unwanted areas in the negative.

A platemaker (figure 17-25) is used to burn or expose the plate. It consists of a vacuum frame, for holding the flat and plate in tight contact, and a light source. Procedures for burning and processing the plate follow:

Place the plate, emulsion side up, on the rubber blanket of the vacuum frame. Position the flat, emulsion side down, on top of the plate. Align the edges of the flat with the edges of the plate.

Close the vacuum frame and turn on the vacuum pump. Once air is evacu-

**Figure 17-26:** Plate developing sink. (NuArc Co., Inc.)

ated, the flat and plate will be held tightly together. Flip the frame over so that the flat and plate face the light source. Set the timer for the desired exposure and burn the plate.

**Caution!** The light source emits ultraviolet light. Do not look directly at the light source. Ultraviolet light can damage your eyes.

The first step in processing is to remove the unexposed light-sensitive coating from the plate. This is done by wiping a small quantity of desensitizer over the plate with a cotton pad.

Place the plate on a clear flat surface. A plate developing sink (figure 17-26) may be used for this purpose.

The second step is to produce a visible image on the plate. Lacquer is used for this purpose. Use a second cotton pad to wipe the lacquer over the image areas.

After processing, wash the excess lacquer from the plate with water. The plate is now ready to be placed on the offset press. If the plate will not be printed immediately, coat its surface with gum arabic. The gum arabic protects the plate and keeps it from oxidizing. A cotton pad may be used to coat the plate.

## SELF CHECK

1. List in their proper sequence the basic steps involved in preparing a direct-image plate.
2. Explain the procedures for preparing a mechanical.
3. List in their proper sequence the basic steps involved in preparing a diffusion-transfer plate.
4. List in their proper sequence the basic steps involved in burning and processing a presensitized plate.

Lithographic plates are printed on:

- Offset duplicators
- Offset presses

Offset duplicators are used for small printing jobs. They print on paper up to 14″ x 20″. A table-top offset duplicator is shown in figure 18-1. A small, floor model is shown in figure 18-2.

Offset presses have more precise controls and systems than duplicators. Offset presses are used to print magazines, books, and newspapers either from sheets (figure 18-3) or from rolls of paper (figure 18-4). A roll-fed press is called a web-fed press.

Although a variety of machines are used to print lithographic plates, they all contain the same operating systems:

- Dampening system
- Inking system
- Feeding and registering system
- Printing system
- Delivery system

**Figure 18-1:** A table-top offset duplicator. (A.B. Dick Co.)

**Figure 18-2:** A floor model offset duplicator. (A.B. Dick Co.)

**Figure 18-3:** A sheet-fed offset press. (Heidelberg Eastern Inc.)

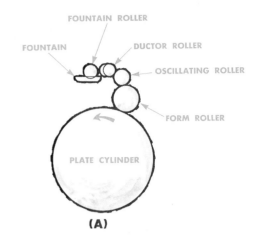

**(A)**

**Figure 18-4:** This press prints on rolls or webs of paper. (R. R. Donnelly & Sons Co.)

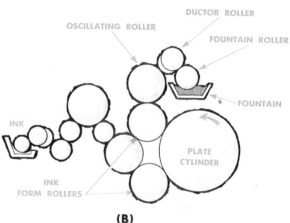

**(B)**

**Figure 18-5:** Two basic techniques are used to coat the non-image area of the plate with water. (A) Conventional technique. (B) Combined technique. Note how in the combined technique some of the same rollers are used to transfer both water and ink to the plate. The water rides on top of the ink. Water transfers to the non-image area of the plate at the same time the ink coats the image area.

The <u>dampening system</u> (figure 18-5) coats the non-image area of the plate with a fountain solution. The fountain solution is basically water. A small amount of commercially-prepared fountain concentrate can be added to produce a mildly acidic solution.

The <u>inking system</u> coats the image area of the plate with ink (figure 18-6). Inks used in lithography are prepared especially for use on offset duplicators and presses. Lithographic inks must

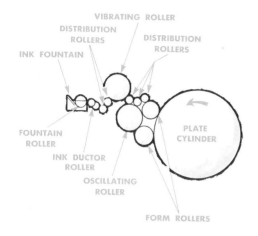

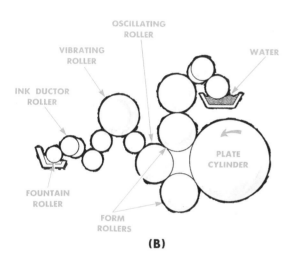

**Figure 18-6:** An inking system is needed to coat the image area of the plate with ink. (A) Conventional technique. (B) Combined technique.

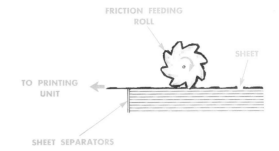

**Figure 18-7:** Friction feeding system for an offset duplicator.

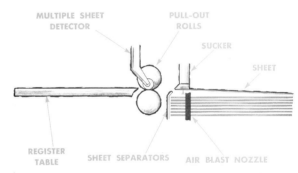

**Figure 18-8:** The feed system on most presses is operated by air-and-vacuum. An air blast lifts sheets from the paper pile. A suction foot (sucker) picks up the top sheet and transfers it to a set of pullout rolls. The pullout rolls pass the sheet to the register table.

not combine with, or absorb, fountain solution.

The feeding and registering system transfers individual sheets of paper from a paper pile into the printing system. Friction (figure 18-7) and air-and-vacuum (figure 18-8) mechanisms are used to transfer sheets from the paper pile.

On the way to the register table, the paper passes through a multiple-sheet detector. This device is used to insure that only one sheet of paper will enter the printing system at a time. The sheet is then conveyed down the register table to a front stop. At this point it is jogged into position before being fed into the printing system.

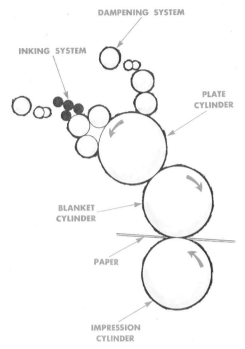

Figure 18-9: A three-cylinder printing system.

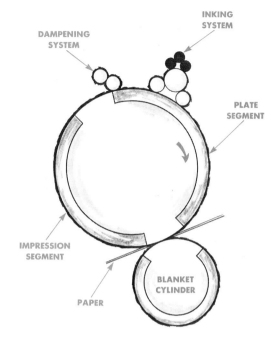

**Figure 18-10:** A two-cylinder printing system. The Davidson duplicator is a two-cylinder machine. (ATF Davidson Co.)

Printing takes place in the <u>printing system</u>. Most press manufacturers make use of a three-cylinder printing system (figure 18-9). The plate on the plate cylinder transfers the image to the blanket. This image is offset onto the paper as it passes between the blanket and impression cylinder. Cylinder grippers are used to carry the paper through the printing system.

In a two-cylinder printing system (figure 18-10), the large, upper cylinder contains a plate segment and an impression segment. The small, lower cylinder holds the blanket. The plate segment on the large cylinder comes in contact with the blanket and transfers the image to it. Paper is not traveling

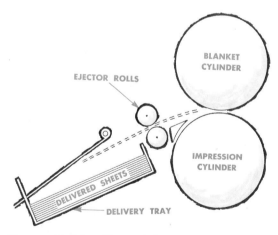

**Figure 18-11:** Chute delivery.

through the printing system at this point. However, when the impression segment of the large cylinder is opposite the blanket, paper passes between the two cylinders and the image offsets onto the sheet.

After receiving the image, the sheet is transferred to a tray or table by the delivery system. Two basic delivery techniques are used. With the chute delivery technique (figure 18-11), the printed sheet is simply ejected into a delivery tray. The ejector rolls help propel the sheet into the tray. With the chain delivery technique (figure 18-12), gripper bars mounted between two chains move the printed sheets from the printing system to a delivery table. The table is automatically lowered as the printed sheets pile up. This type of delivery table is called a receding stacker.

There are many different models of offset duplicators. Operating controls and procedures differ from one model to the next. Study the instruction manual supplied by the manufacturer of your machine for specific operating instructions.

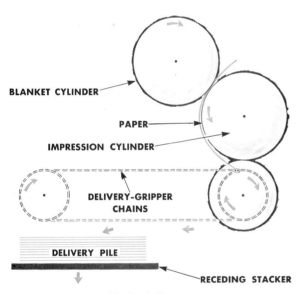

**Figure 18-12:** Chain delivery.

### SELF CHECK

1. List the names of the five operating systems that comprise an offset duplicator.
2. Prepare simple diagrams to illustrate the "friction" and "air-and-vacuum" feeding techniques used on offset duplicators,
3. Using simple diagrams, illustrate the differences between two- and three-cylinder printing systems. Label each of the parts shown.
4. Describe the difference between chute delivery and chain delivery.

# 5    PRINTING WITH A STENCIL

Many items are printed by forcing ink through openings or holes in a stencil (figure V-1). Printing by means of a stencil is generally referred to as screen-process printing. Another common name for this method is silk screen printing. Openings in the stencil control what will be printed on the paper below.

A stencil is nothing more than a thin sheet of paper, film, or other material that has been perforated with lettering or a design. Stencils may be hand-cut from paper or film, prepared photographically, or they may be painted directly on the screen. A type of stencil you probably are already familiar with is shown in figure V-2.

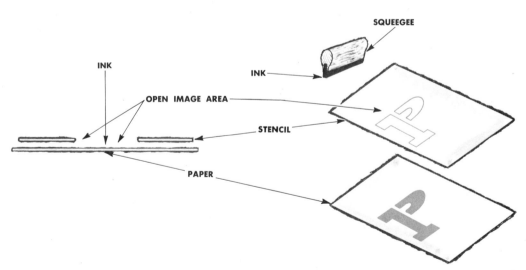

**Figure V-1:**   Screen-process printing.  A squeegee is used to force ink onto the paper through holes in a stencil.

**Figure V-2:** A stencil used for hand lettering.

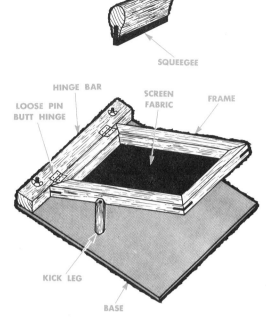

**Figure V-3:** A frame with woven screen material stretched across it serves as the printing press.

The frame (figure V-3) serves as the printing press in screen-process printing. The stencil must be adhered to a screen. The screen is a piece of woven material stretched tightly across a wooden or metal frame. Silk, nylon, dacron, and stainless steel mesh are the materials most often used.

The screen-process of printing is shown in figure V-4. Paper is placed under the printing screen. Ink is applied to the top of the screen. Printing takes place by spreading and forcing the ink through the stencil openings with a rubber squeegee.

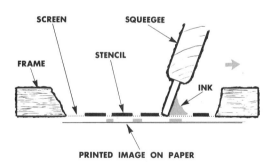

**Figure V-4:** Ink is forced through a stencil that has been adhered to a screen. The ink creates a printed image on the paper.

The stencil serves as the plate in screen-process printing. The shape of the openings in the stencil determine the shape of the image that is printed. The four most commonly used types of stencils are:

- Hand-cut paper stencils
- Hand-cut film stencils
- Photographic stencils
- Hand-painted stencils

Hand-painted stencils are used by artists and will not be discussed in this book. Paper stencils are the easiest to prepare.

Paper stencils are used for short printing runs of less than 100 impressions. Designs must be kept simple. Avoid designs with loose centers such as the letter "O". A silhouette like the one shown in figure 19-1 can be printed with a paper stencil.

Cut a piece of brown wrapping paper slightly smaller than the outside dimensions of the screen frame. Draw the outline of the image to be printed directly on the paper. Use carbon paper to transfer an already prepared design.

Place the stencil paper on a piece of smooth cardboard or a glass plate, and use a sharp stencil knife or single-edge razor blade to cut the design (figure 19-2). Do not remove the cutouts at this time.

Transfer the cut stencil to the base of a clean screen printing frame. Lower the screen and position the stencil as required.

Adhere the stencil to the screen fabric by running a bead of ink across

**Figure 19-1:** Silhouette designs can be readily converted into hand-cut stencils.

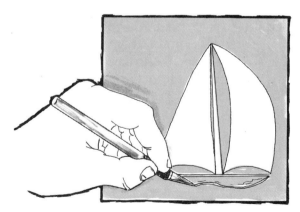

**Figure 19-2:** Cutting a paper stencil.

**Figure 19-3:** Adhering the paper stencil to a screen.

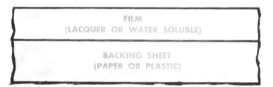

**Figure 19-4:** The two layers of a piece of hand-cut stencil film.

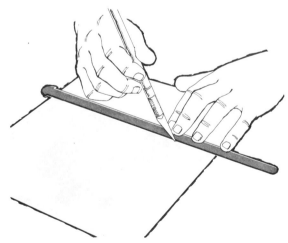

**Figure 19-5:** A piece of stencil film has been taped to this design in preparation for cutting.

the screen with a squeegee (figure 19-3). The ink serves as an adhesive. The stencil can be printed after the cutouts are removed from the underside of the screen.

Hand-cut film stencils are quite durable. Many thousands of impressions can be made from a single stencil. Appropriate designs include poster-size lettering and pictures that do not contain fine detail.

Hand-cut film stencils (figure 19-4) are made from a thin layer of lacquer or water-soluble based material on a paper or plastic backing sheet.

Lacquer and water-soluble films are prepared in the same way. Different solvents and inks must be used to adhere and print each type of film. Lacquer films are adhered with lacquer thinner, and can be used with water- and oil-base inks. Lacquer-base inks cannot be used with lacquer stencils. Water-soluble films are adhered with water, and can be used with oil- and lacquer-base inks. Water-base inks cannot be used with water-soluble stencils.

Choose a piece of stencil film that is larger than the design. Place the stencil film over the design, film side up, and tape it in place. The design should be visible through the stencil film (figure 19-5). Use a sharp stencil knife or single-edge razor blade. Cut through the film layer only. Do not cut into the backing sheet.

The film is stripped from the backing sheet after each area of the design is cut. Use the point of your knife to peel the film from the backing (figure 19-6). Be careful to remove only those parts

**Figure 19-6:** Removing the unwanted film from the image areas of the stencil.

**Figure 19-7:** Adhering the stencil to the screen.

of the film that will form the image during printing.

Lacquer film is adhered to the screen with lacquer thinner. Water-soluble film is adhered with water or with a mixture of water and alcohol. Be sure to use the adhering solution recommended by the film's manufacturer.

Place the stencil, film side up, on a pad of newspaper. Place a clean screen over the stencil. The stencil is now ready to be adhered. Two cotton cloths are used for this purpose. Dampen one cloth with the required adherent.

Start at one corner of the stencil and press the dampened pad against the film. Moisten 4 to 6 square inches of the film's surface. This softens the film and causes it to stick to the screen fabric. Now quickly wipe the area of the stencil that was just adhered with the dry cloth. Repeat until the entire stencil is adhered.

A film stencil in the process of being adhered is pictured in figure 19-7. Note that the adhered area is darker in color than the area that has not been adhered. Light spots on the stencil indicate improper adhesion. A properly adhered stencil will have a uniform color.

Allow the film stencil to dry before removing the stencil backing (figure 19-8). A fan may be used to shorten the drying time.

**Figure 19-8:** Removing the backing sheet from the hand-cut stencil.

Photographic stencils can be used to reproduce fine detail. There are two types of photographic stencils, direct and indirect. Both types are prepared in much the same way.

Indirect stencils are prepared by contact printing through a film positive onto a light-sensitive stencil material. After processing, the stencil is adhered to a screen.

Positives are usually prepared in one of two ways. They can be made by drawing an india ink image on tracing paper. They can also be prepared photographically by contact printing a negative on a piece of process film.

A platemaker (figure 19-9) can be used to expose the stencil. It consists of a vacuum frame for holding the film positive and stencil material in tight contact, and a light source located in the platemaker's base.

**Figure 19-9:** A platemaker is used to expose the indirect photographic stencil.

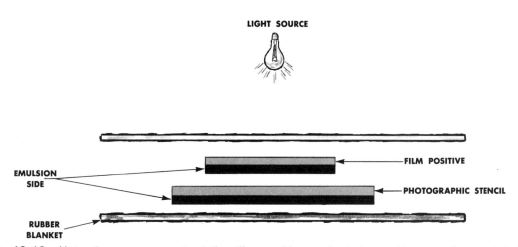

**Figure 19-10:** Note the arrangement of the film positive and photographic stencil material during exposure. Exposure is made through the back of the positive and the back of the stencil.

The stencil material consists of a light-sensitive emulsion on a plastic backing. Place it, emulsion side down, on the rubber blanket of the vacuum frame. Position the film positive, emulsion (readable) side down on top of the stencil (figure 19-10).

Close the vacuum frame and turn on the vacuum pump. Once the air is evacuated the positive and stencil will be held tightly together. Flip the vacuum frame over. Set the timer for the correct exposure and expose the stencil.

Light passing through the clear areas of the film positive will harden the stencil's emulsion. Because no light passes through the opaque areas of the positive, the emulsion behind these areas will remain soft.

**Safety Note.** The light source of the platemaker emits ultraviolet light. Do

not look directly at the light source. Ultraviolet light can damage your eyes.

After exposure, remove the stencil material from the vacuum frame and place it, emulsion side up, into a tray of stencil developer. Develop the stencil for the recommended time (figure 19-11).

Now remove the stencil from the developer. Note that it does not yet contain a visible image. The image becomes visible during the washout operation that follows development.

Place the stencil, emulsion side up, in a sink. Wash away all of the unexposed (image) areas of the stencil with running water. The temperature of the water should be set to the washout temperature recommended by the manufacturer. After washout, allow the stencil to sit in a bath of cold water for approximately one minute.

An indirect stencil must be adhered to the screen immediately after the washout. Place the stencil, emulsion side up, on a pad of newspaper, and position a clean screen over the stencil.

Use paper towels to absorb the excess moisture from the stencil. Start at one corner of the screen and blot the stencil (figure 19-12). Continue blotting until all of the excess moisture has been absorbed from the stencil.

Allow the emulsion of the stencil to dry thoroughly before removing the backing sheet. A fan may be used to shorten the drying time.

Direct photographic stencils are prepared directly on the screen fabric. The screen is coated with a light-sensitive emulsion then exposed through a film positive to a source of light. Fol-

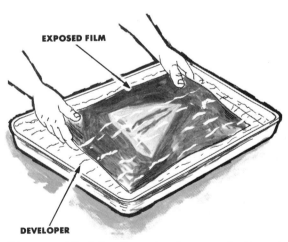

**Figure 19-11:** Developing an indirect photographic stencil.

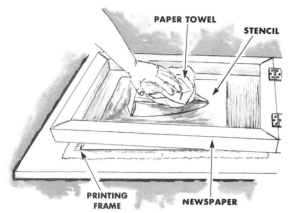

**Figure 19-12:** Adhere the indirect stencil to the screen by blotting with paper towels. Be sure and change towels when they become too damp to absorb additional moisture.

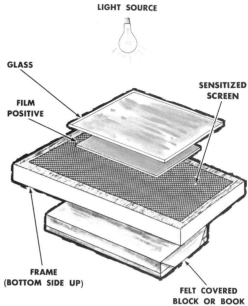

**Figure 19-13:** The film positive and sensitized screen must remain in tight contact during exposure. The weight of the glass helps to maintain the required contact.

low the manufacturer's recommendations when mixing commercially-prepared emulsions and sensitizers.

During exposure the film positive and screen must remain in tight contact. One method of maintaining contact between the positive and screen is shown in figure 19-13. Photoflood lamps, fluorescent tubes, carbon arc lights, and direct sunlight can all be used to expose the emulsion.

## SELF CHECK

1. List in their proper sequence the basic steps involved in cutting and adhering a paper stencil.

2. List in their proper sequence the basic steps involved in cutting and adhering a hand-cut film stencil.
3. Describe the major difference between an indirect and direct photographic stencil.
4. List in their proper sequence the steps involved in exposing and processing an indirect photographic stencil.

The hand-operated screen-process press is used for short printing runs. Power-operated presses are used for long runs. Specially designed machines have been developed to print on a variety of shapes and kinds of objects.

The basic parts of a hand-operated press (figure 20-1) are the frame, screen fabric, base, and squeegee. The <u>frame</u> (figure 20-2) is usually made from wood. <u>Screens</u> can be made of polyester, silk, nylon, dacron, or stainless steel mesh. Silk and polyester are the most popular fabrics for screen-process printing. The <u>base</u> serves as a surface on which to locate and hold the paper to be printed. It is fastened to the frame with loose-pin butt hinges. The <u>squeegee</u> is used to force ink through the stencil. It consists of a hard-rubber blade held in a wooden handle.

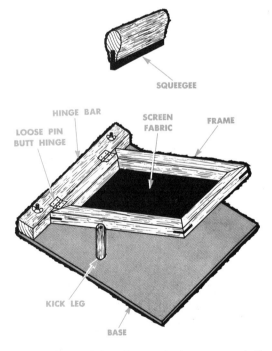

**Figure 20-1:** A hand-operated screen printing press with its major parts labeled.

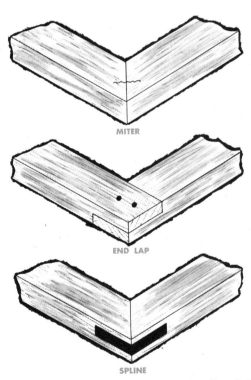

**Figure 20-2:** Miter, end lap, and spline joints can be used to hold the sides of the frame together.

**Figure 20-3:** Use a cardboard squeegee to cover the non-printing areas of the screen with a thin layer of blockout.

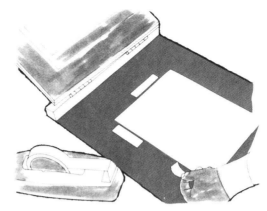

**Figure 20-4:** Registration guides are used to position the paper prior to printing.

Non-printing areas around the stencil must be <u>masked</u> or <u>blocked out</u> before printing can begin (figure 20-3). Tape strips of paper to the bottom of the screen with masking tape in order to block out the large non-printing areas. Liquid blockout may also be used. Blockout is applied to the screen with a cardboard squeegee. Cover the non-printing areas only.

Setting registration guides is the next step in the printing process. Place a sheet of paper of the correct size on the base of the printing frame. Position it according to the location of the stencil image. Raise the screen and mark the paper's location.

Short leads or strips of chip board may be used as registration guides. Fasten these guides to the base with masking tape (figure 20-4).

The screen is then inked. Use a spatula to run a bead of ink along one

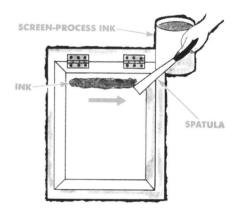

**Figure 20-5:** Inking the screen with a spatula.

edge of the stencil (figure 20-5). Apply enough ink to make several prints.

Printing can now begin. Raise the frame and place a sheet of paper against the registration guides. Lower the frame and pull the ink across the stencil with the edge of the squeegee (figure 20-6).

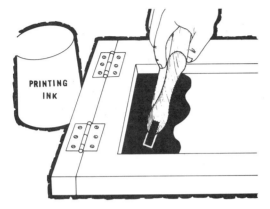

**Figure 20-6:** Hold the squeegee firmly. Keep it at a sixty degree angle with the screen.

**Figure 20-7:** A rack used for drying screen-process prints. (Advance Process Supply Co.)

Raise the frame and remove the print from the baseboard. Place the print on a rack to dry (figure 20-7). Additional copies are printed by repeating the above procedures.

All ink must be removed from the screen, squeegee, and spatula before it dries. The blockout and stencil must also be removed. To remove the ink, cover the baseboard with several sheets of newspaper. Scoop up the excess ink on the screen with a piece of cardboard and return it to the ink can. Also use the cardboard to scrape excess ink from the squeegee and spatula.

Pour a small quantity of a suitable ink solvent on the screen. Use water for a water-base ink, lacquer thinner for a lacquer-base ink, and mineral spirits for an oil-base ink. Wipe the screen, squeegee and spatula clean with a cloth moistened in this solvent.

A solvent is used to remove the blockout. Water is used to remove water-base masking material. Lacquer thinner is used to remove lacquer-base blockout.

Hand-cut water-soluble stencils and indirect photographic stencils are removed by holding the screen under hot running water. Direct photographic stencils must be removed from the screen with a special solvent. Follow the emulsion manufacturer's recommendations regarding stencil removal.

Lacquer film stencils are removed with lacquer thinner. Place a pad of newspaper beneath the frame, and pour a small amount of lacquer thinner on the stencil. After the stencil has had a chance to soak, rub the top of the screen with a clean cloth. As the stencil dissolves it will stick to the newspaper.

A power-operated flat-bed screen printing press is shown in figure 20-8.

**Figure 20-8:** Power-operated screen printing press. (Jos. E. Podgor Co., Inc.)

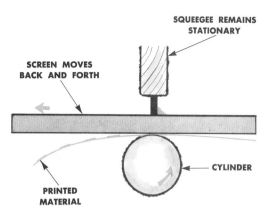

**Figure 20-10:** Operating principle of a cylinder press. The screen containing the stencil moves over a cylinder that carries the material to be printed. A vacuum holds the printed material in contact with the cylinder. The squeegee is held stationary during printing, while the material to be printed moves forward at the same speed as the screen.

**Figure 20-9:** Automatic screen-process cylinder press with automatic feeding unit. (General Research, Inc.)

The raising and lowering of the screen and the action of the squeegee is mechanized on this type of press. Some power-operated presses are also equipped with automatic feed and delivery systems.

A cylinder-type screen printing press is shown in figure 20-9. Its operating principle is illustrated in figure 20-10.

## SELF CHECK

1. Sketch a picture of a hand-operated screen printing press. Label each of its major parts.
2. List in their proper sequence the basic steps to be followed when printing with a hand-operated screen printing press.
3. Prepare a chart which illustrates the proper solvent to be used with each of the following materials: water-base ink, lacquer-base ink, oil-base ink, water-base blockout, lacquer-base blockout, hand-cut stencils, and photographic stencils.
4. Outline the procedures for removing a lacquer film stencil from the screen fabric.

# 6 FINISHING AND BINDING

Finishing and binding operations usually follow printing. Cutting, folding, and gathering of printed sheets are the most common finishing operations. Other finishing techniques include scoring, perforating, drilling, embossing, and die cutting.

The most common binding methods are: saddle-wire, side-wire, sewn soft-cover, sewn case-bound, and adhesive, mechanical and loose-leaf binding. Each of these techniques are discussed in this part of the book.

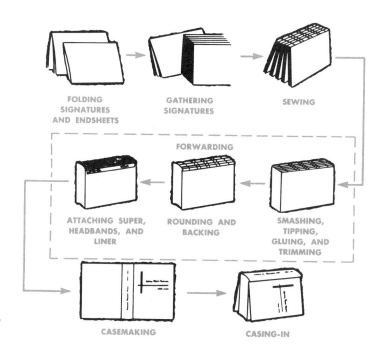

FOLDING SIGNATURES AND ENDSHEETS

GATHERING SIGNATURES

SEWING

FORWARDING

ATTACHING SUPER, HEADBANDS, AND LINER

ROUNDING AND BACKING

SMASHING, TIPPING, GLUING, AND TRIMMING

CASEMAKING

CASING-IN

Finishing refers to several operations that may be performed on printed material after it has left the press. The most common finishing operations are:

- Cutting
- Folding
- Gathering

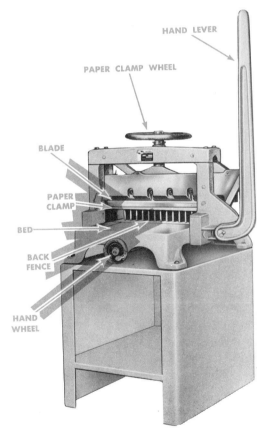

Figure 21-1: Hand-lever "guillotine" paper cutter with major parts labeled. (Challenge Machinery Co.)

Cutting is usually done with a paper cutter. A hand-lever paper cutter is shown in figure 21-1. A power-driven model is pictured in figure 21-2. Both of these cutters are of the guillotine type. The size of a paper cutter is designated by the maximum width of paper it can cut.

**Safety Notes.** Secure permission before using the paper cutter. Only one person should operate this machine at a time. Keep both hands away from the blade.

Hand- and power-driven paper cutters are operated in essentially the same way. Begin by moving the back fence to obtain the desired depth of cut. The front handwheel is used for this purpose. The distance between the

Figure 21-2: Hydraulic power-driven paper cutter. (Mohawk Paper Mills, Inc.)

blade and fence is indicated by a measuring tape or a scale built into the bed of the machine.

Jog the paper and place it on the cutter. Position the paper pile against the back fence and the left side of the cutter.

Place a strip of chip board directly below the blade, under the paper pile. The chip board helps protect the cutting stick which it covers. Place another strip of chip board on top of the paper and directly below the paper clamp. This strip keeps the top sheets of paper from being damaged by the clamp.

Lower the clamp by turning the top wheel to the right. The clamp should press the paper tightly against the bed of the cutter.

Use both hands to activate the cutter blade. Some hand-lever cutters have a safety pin which must be held with one hand while the other hand pulls on the lever. Others require the operator to grasp the lever with two hands. Power cutters are usually equipped with controls that must be operated with both hands.

After completing the cut raise the blade. Check to be sure the safety device on the cutter is working. Then raise the paper clamp and remove the paper. Repeat the above process to obtain the other desired dimensions.

**Safety Note.** Always adjust the paper clamp to its lowest position when leaving the cutter area. Be sure to turn off the power on power-driven machines.

<u>Folding</u> is done by hand, with a bone folder, or with folding machines. An

**Figure 21-3:** A table top folder is used to fold letters and brochures. (MBM Corp.)

**Figure 21-4:** This folder is capable of producing book and magazine signatures. (Heidelberg-Eastern, Inc.)

office folding machine is shown in figure 21-3. It is used to fold small sheets of paper. A large folder capable of producing book and magazine signatures is shown in figure 21-4. A <u>signature</u> is a sheet of paper that has been folded a number of times, then trimmed with a paper cutter to form pages. Several paper folds are illustrated in figure 21-5.

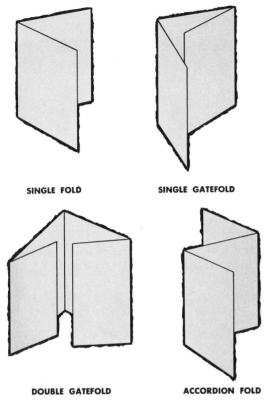

**SINGLE FOLD**   **SINGLE GATEFOLD**

**DOUBLE GATEFOLD**   **ACCORDION FOLD**

**Figure 21-5:** Several of the common paper folds.

**Figure 21-6:** A collator is used to assemble single sheets of paper or signatures in their proper sequence for binding. (Challenge Machinery Co.)

Assembling sheets or signatures in their proper sequence prior to binding is called "gathering." This may be done by hand or by machine. Machines used for this purpose are called collators. A small desk-top collator is shown in figure 21-6.

## SELF CHECK

1. Define the term "finishing" and name three "finishing operations".
2. List five procedures that relate to the safe operation of a guillotine paper cutter.
3. Outline the procedures to follow when cutting paper with a guillotine paper cutter.
4. Define "gathering."

Sheets of paper may be bound together in several ways. The most common methods are:

- Saddle-wire
- Side-wire
- Sewn soft-cover
- Sewn case-bound
- Adhesive
- Mechanical
- Loose-leaf

Saddle-wire binding is illustrated in figure 22-1. Wire staples are used as the fastening device. The staples pass through the back of several pages that have been assembled and folded. Materials bound in this manner will lie flat when open.

Side-wire binding is illustrated in figure 22-2. Again wire staples are used as the fastening device. This time, however, the staples pass through one edge of the assembled pages. Generally, materials bound in this manner will not lie flat and have to be held open.

The sewn soft-cover binding method is illustrated in figure 22-3. Binding thread is used as the fastening device. The thread is sewn through holes punched in the center fold of a signature or through one edge of an assembled pile of pages. Several signatures may be sewn together using this techinque.

The sewn case-bound method of binding is illustrated in figure 22-4.

**Figure 22-1:** Saddle-wire binding. Materials bound in this manner lie flat when open.

**Figure 22-2:** Side-wire binding. Materials bound in this manner do not lie flat and have to be held open.

**Figure 22-3:** Sewn soft-cover binding. Binding thread is used to hold the pages or signatures together.

**Figure 22-4:** Case binding. Books bound in this manner will stand up under hard use.

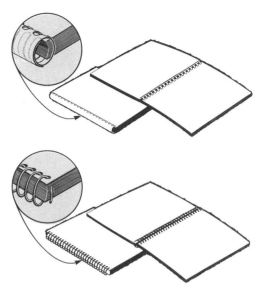

**Figure 22-6:** Mechanical binding is accomplished with plastic combs and with wire springs.

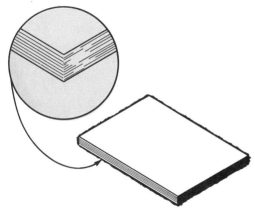

**Figure 22-5:** Adhesive or perfect binding. Sheets of paper are held together by a flexible adhesive.

**Figure 22-7:** A mechanical binding machine is used to punch the paper and insert the plastic combs. (General Binding Corp.)

Individual signatures are first sewn together with binding thread. Sewn signatures are then encased between hard covers made from binders board and cloth.

Perfect binding and padding are other names for adhesive binding. An adhesive or padding compound holds the assembled sheets together. Adhesive binding is illustrated in figure 22-5.

Notepads, telephone books, and pocketbooks are among the products that are bound in this manner.

**Figure 22-8:** Binding post type of loose-leaf binding.

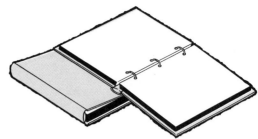

**Figure 22-9:** A ring binder is also used for loose-sheet binding.

<u>Mechanical bindings</u> such as plastic combs and wire springs are also used to fasten sheets of paper together. These are inserted through holes punched along one edge of an assembled pile of paper. Both types of mechanical binding are illustrated in figure 22-6. A machine used for punching paper and inserting plastic combs is pictured in figure 22-7.

<u>Loose-leaf binding</u> methods allow for the addition or removal of pages from the bound material. Post and ring binders are used. The post type of loose-leaf binding is illustrated in figure 22-8. A ring binder is shown in figure 22-9.

## SELF CHECK

1. Explain what is meant by the term "binding".
2. List the names of seven methods used to bind paper together.
3. Prepare a chart describing the characteristics of the binding methods discussed in this unit. Include simple diagrams to illustrate these methods.
4. What is "perfect" binding?

# ABOUT PAPER AND INK

# 7

Many types of materials can be printed on. Plastic, glass, and fabric are just some. However, by far the most important material is paper.

Ink is also an important ingredient in the printing process. It is ink that transfers from plate to paper to form the printed image.

Ts'ai Lun, a Chinese court official, invented paper. He did this nearly 1900 years ago in 105 A.D. Today, well over 400 pounds of paper is used each year by every man, woman, and child in America.

Making paper by hand is an excellent way to learn papermaking procedures. Extensive equipment and materials are not required.

Equipment includes a tub or large pail and a mold and deckle. These items are shown in figure 23-1. The mold is a wooden frame covered with metal screening. The deckle is a frame that is the same size as the mold. Other items needed are an egg beater, rolling pin, electric iron, blotting

**Figure 23-2:** Beating the pulp mixture.

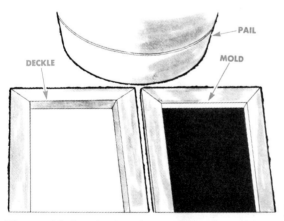

**Figure 23-1:** A tub or large pail and a mold and deckle are needed to make paper by hand.

paper, instant laundry starch, and a box of soft facial tissues.

Fill the tub with warm water. Shred about thirty tissues into the water. Do not use the "wet strength" kind. Tissues serve as a substitute for wood pulp. Wood pulp can be used, if it is available.

Add one tablespoon of instant laundry starch to two cups of water. Pour this mixture into the tub. The starch serves to size or fill the pores of the paper. Beat the pulp mixture with an egg beater until it is free of lumps (figure 23-2).

The sheet of paper can now be formed. Place the deckle over the mold

**Figure 23-3:** Slide the deckle and mold, deckle side up, into the pulp mixture. Then level the deckle and mold and lift it from the mixture.

**Figure 23-4:** Transfer the newly made sheet of paper from the mold to a sheet of blotting paper.

and slide both into the pulp mixture (figure 23-3). After leveling the deckle and mold assembly, lift it carefully from the mixture.

Transfer the newly made sheet of paper to a piece of blotting paper (figure 23-4). Cover the paper with a second blotter and press out the excess water with a rolling pin. Then press

with an electric iron. Do this while the sheet is still between the blotting papers. You have just made a sheet of paper by hand.

Modern paper manufacturing techniques are similar to those used to make paper by hand. The key steps in the processing of wood pulp and the making of paper are shown in figure 23-

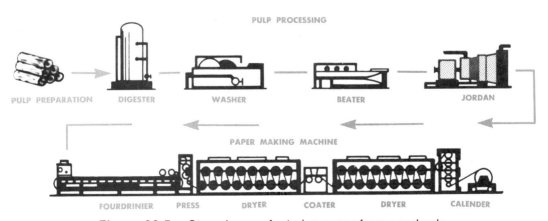

**Figure 23-5:** Steps in manufacturing paper from wood pulp.

**Figure 23-6:** Hammermill Paper Company's main mill and general offices occupy a 225 acre tract of land. Approximately 2,000 persons are employed here. The mill produces over 280,000,000 pounds of paper each year. (Hammermill Paper Co.)

**Figure 23-7:** A Fourdrinier papermaking machine. The pulp mixture is poured onto the wire screen. As the screen moves forward it also shakes sideways. This serves to weave and mat the fibers together as the water drains off. (Bergstrom Paper Co.)

| COMMON KINDS OF PAPER | | | |
|---|---|---|---|
| **KIND OF PAPER** | **SOME GENERAL USES** | **BASIC SIZE (INCHES)** | **BASIS WEIGHTS (POUNDS)** |
| BOND | STATIONARY, BUSINESS FORMS, DIRECT-MAIL ADVERTISING | 17 x 22 | 9, 13, 16, 20, 24 |
| BOOK | BOOKS, PAMPHLETS, BROCHURES, DIRECT-MAIL ADVERTISING | 25 x 38 | 50, 60, 70, 80, 90, 100 |
| COVER | COVERS FOR BOOKLETS, BINDERS, ANNOUNCEMENTS | 20 x 26 | 50, 60, 65, 80, 90, 100 |
| BRISTOL | INDEX CARDS, POSTCARDS, TICKETS, BOOKLET COVERS | 25 1/2 x 30 1/2 | 90, 110, 140, 170 |
| NEWSPRINT | NEWSPAPERS, DIRECT-MAIL ADVERTISING | 24 x 36 | 32, 34 |
| DUPLICATOR | SPIRIT-DUPLICATED MATERIALS | 17 x 22 | 16, 20, 24 |
| MIMEOGRAPH | MIMEOGRAPHED MATERIALS | 17 x 22 | 16, 20, 24 |

**Figure 23-8:** Common kinds of paper.

5. Major differences lie in the preparation of the pulp and the mechanization of the papermaking process. A typical papermaking plant is pictured in figure 23-6. A huge papermaking machine is shown in figure 23-7.

Some common kinds of printing papers are bond, book, cover, bristol, newsprint, duplicator and mimeograph. Uses for each kind of paper and information concerning their basic size and basis weight is provided in figure 23-8.

"Basic size" refers to the standard sheet size used by the paper mill to compute the weight of each kind of paper. The basic size is not the same for all kinds of paper.

"Basis weight" refers to the weight of a ream (500 sheets) of paper cut to its basic size. Paper is often referred to in terms of its basis or ream weight: 20-pound bond, 50-pound book, etc. Many kinds of paper are available in several different basis weights.

## SELF CHECK

1. Describe how to make paper by hand.
2. Use simple diagrams to illustrate the key steps in the paper manufacturing process.
3. Describe what is meant by the terms basic size and basis weight.
4. Name seven kinds of paper, and list how each is used.

Ink is transferred from plate to paper during printing. It is ink that forms the image on the printed product.

Most printing inks consist of three components: a pigment, a vehicle, and one or more modifiers. The pigment provides ink with its color. Many pigment colors are produced from rocks and clays. Others can be traced back to plants, sea life, and even insects.

The vehicle is the fluid component that carries the pigment. Oil, lacquer, and water are three important vehicles.

Modifiers are ingredients that provide the ink with certain desired characteristics. For example, driers may be added to speed up the drying process.

Key steps in the manufacture of printing inks are shown in figure 24-1.

**Figure 24-2:** An ink mixer is used to blend the pigment, modifiers, and vehicle together. (National Association of Printing Ink Manufacturers, Inc.)

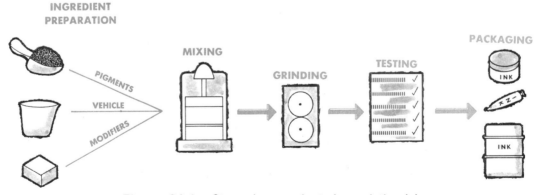

**Figure 24-1:** Steps in manufacturing printing inks.

During the preparation step ingredients are selected and processed in preparation for mixing.

An ink mixer is shown in figure 24-2. It is the job of this machine to blend the ingredients together.

The blended mixture is transferred to a mill or grinder (figure 24-3). This machine further reduces the size of the solid particles in the mixture.

Next, the ink is tested to insure that it will behave as it is supposed to under actual printing conditions.

Packaging is the final step. Inks may be packaged in tubes, cans, or drums. Tank trucks are needed to deliver ink to large users such as newspaper and magazine printing plants.

Each printing process requires the use of an ink developed specifically for that process. Letterpress inks are designed to distribute evenly over raised plate surfaces. Gravure inks must be fluid and should dry rapidly. Lithographic inks are formulated so they do not mix with the fountain solution. Inks used for screen-process printing must have the consistency of a thick paint.

Another thing to consider is the eventual use of the printed item. The ink on items used outdoors must be able to withstand the weather. Ink printed on fabrics should hold up under repeated washings. Products that will be handled by very young children must be printed with nontoxic inks.

**Figure 24-3:** A mill is used to grind the solid particles in the ink mixture and distribute them throughout the vehicle. (National Association of Printing Ink Manufacturers, Inc.)

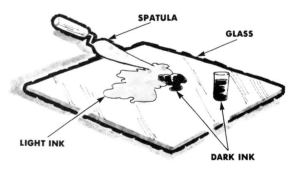

**Figure 24-4:** In the school shop, ink is usually mixed on a glass slab with a spatula. Add very small quantities of ink and mix thoroughly before adding more ink.

In the school shop two or more inks can be mixed together on a slab of glass to obtain a desired ink color. A spatula is used to mix the inks (figure 24-4).

**SELF CHECK**

1. Define the term "pigment" and list five sources from which pigments are obtained.
2. Describe what is meant by the term "vehicle" and list 3 types of vehicles.
3. Prepare an outline of the key steps in the manufacture of printing inks.
4. Explain why you should consider the eventual use of a printed item before selecting the ink to be used in printing that item.

# GLOSSARY

**Basic size:** The standard sheet size, in inches, used to compute the weight of each kind of paper.

**Basis weight:** The weight, in pounds, of a ream of paper cut to its basic size.

**Bind:** To fasten pages of a book together with wire staples, thread, adhesive or other means.

**Blanket cylinder:** The cylinder on an offset press which receives the inked image from the plate cylinder and transfers it to the paper.

**Brayer:** A handled roller used to ink type forms prior to proofing.

**California job case:** A storage case which contains a complete font of foundry type.

**Centering:** Setting type so that all lines are ragged left and ragged right and have a common center line.

**Clip art:** Preprinted illustrations in sheet and book form. These illustrations are used to add clarity or interest to a visual message.

**Cold-type composition:** Setting type by photographic or mechanical means other than hot metal.

**Comprehensive layout:** A prototype of a product to be printed. It contains more detail than a rough layout.

**Contact screen:** Screen containing dots with fuzzy edges used to form a dot pattern on negatives made from continuous-tone prints.

**Continuous-tone copy:** Copy containing blacks, whites, and shades of grey. A black and white photograph is an example.

**Copy:** Any material to be reproduced by printing including type-written manuscript, photographs, and artwork.

**Display type:** Type that is larger than fourteen points.

**Duplicate plates:** Plates that are made from original letterpress plates. Stereotypes, electrotypes, and rubber plates are duplicate letterpress plates.

**Em:** A spacing unit equal to the square of the type size being used.

**Finishing:** Several types of operations that may be performed on a printed material after it has left the press. Cutting, folding, gathering, scoring, perforating, drilling, embossing, and die cutting are all finishing operations.

**Flat:** An assembly of photographic negatives or positives in position on a goldenrod support. Presensitized lithographic plates are exposed through the flat.

**Flush left:** All lines of type are aligned with the left margin and are ragged right.

**Flush right:** All lines of type are aligned with the right margin and are ragged left.

**Font:** An assortment of type of one size and style including upper and lowercase letters, figures, and punctuation marks.

**Foundry type:** Type cast in individual pieces and stored in California job cases. A composing stick is used to set foundry type.

**Furniture:** Wood or metal blocks used when locking type forms in a chase.

**Galley:** A three-sided metal tray.

**Gauge pin:** A metal pin used to hold sheets in position on the tympan of a platen press.

**Gravure printing:** Printing from a recessed surface. Also called intaglio printing.

**Halftone:** A reproduction of continuous-tone copy formed by printed dots of various sizes.

**Hot-type composition:** Setting type with metal characters cast from a mold. Foundry type, monotype, and linotype are examples of hot type.

**Ink:** The material that forms the image on the paper that is printed. Ink usually consists of a pigment, a vehicle, and modifiers.

**Justification:** The spacing out of a line of type so that it fills the full measure to which the type is being set. All lines begin at the left margin and end at the right margin.

**Leading:** Spacing used between lines of type.

**Letterpress printing:** Printing from a raised surface. Also called relief printing.

**Line copy:** Copy containing only blacks and whites. There are no grey tones.

**Line gage:** A measuring instrument used by printers.

**Linotype:** A machine which casts slugs or lines of type from assembled matrices.

**Lithography:** Printing from a flat surface. Lithography is based on the principle that oil and water do not mix.

**Measure:** The length to which a line of type is set.

**Mechanical:** The pasteup used as camera-ready copy in line and halftone photography.

**Paper:** A substance on which copy is either written or printed. Paper is normally made from wood or rag fibers.

**Photoengraving:** A relief printing plate made by a photo-mechanical process. Non-image areas are etched below the surface of the plate.

**Phototypesetter:** A cold-type composing machine used to set type by contact or projection printing on film or paper.

**Pica:** Printer's unit of measurement equal to one-sixth of an inch.

**Plates:** Image carriers used in the various printing processes to transfer ink to the paper.

**Point system:** Printer's system of measurement based on the point. There are 72 points in an inch and 12 points in a pica.

**Printing:** The process of transferring an image from a plate onto paper or some other material.

**Process camera:** A camera used to expose line and halftone negatives.

**Proof press:** A machine used to pull proofs of type forms and other letterpress plates.

**Proofreader's marks:** Symbols used in proofreading to indicate changes to be made in the copy.

**Quoins:** Wedge-shaped devices used to lock a type form in a chase.

**Ream:** Five hundred sheets of paper.

**Reproduction proof (repro):** A proof made from a type form that is suitable for use as camera copy.

**Screen-process printing:** Printing by passing ink through openings in a stencil.

**Signature:** A sheet of paper that has been folded a number of times to yield a desired number of pages.

**Stripping:** Positioning and attaching negatives or positives to a flat prior to platemaking.

**Squeegee:** A hard rubber blade projecting from a wooden handle. It is used to spread ink across the stencil in screen-process printing.

**Thermography:** Technique used to raise the image on a freshly printed product by coating it with a resin powder and applying heat.

**Thumbnail sketch:** A crude sketch of the elements that will be included in a printed job. Thumbnail sketches are used to explore possible designs for the product.

**Type-high:** The standard height of type used in letterpress printing. Type-high in the United States is .918 inch.

**Type size:** The size in points of the body of a piece of hot type. The distance in points from the top of ascender letters to the bottom of descender letters in cold type.

**Typewriter composition:** Setting cold type with a standard or proportional spacing typewriter.

# INDEX